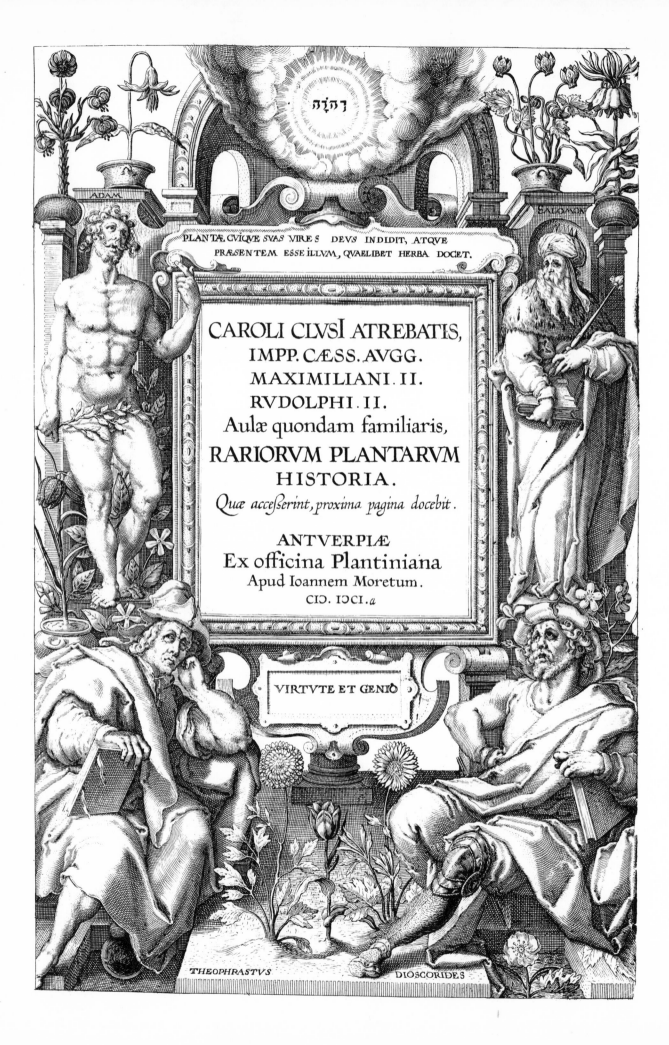

יהוה

ADAM · SALOMON

PLANTÆ CVIQVE SVAS VIRES DEVS INDIDIT, ATQVE
PRÆSENTEM ESSE ILLVM, QVAELIBET HERBA DOCET.

CAROLI CLVSI ATREBATIS,
IMPP. CÆSS. AVGG.
MAXIMILIANI. II.
RVDOLPHI. II.
Aulæ quondam familiaris,
RARIORVM PLANTARVM
HISTORIA.
Quæ accesserint, proxima pagina docebit.

ANTVERPIÆ
Ex officina Plantiniana
Apud Ioannem Moretum.
CIƆ. IƆCI.a

VIRTVTE ET GENIO

THEOPHRASTVS   DIOSCORIDES

Plant and Floral Woodcuts for Designers and Craftsmen

*419 Illustrations
from the Renaissance Herbal of*
Carolus Clusius

*Selected and Arranged by
Theodore Menten*

Dover Publications, Inc., New York

Published in Canada by General Publishing Company, Ltd., 30 Lesmill Road, Don Mills, Toronto, Ontario.
Published in the United Kingdom by Constable and Company, Ltd., 10 Orange Street, London WC 2.

Plant and Floral Woodcuts for Designers and Craftsmen is a new work, first published by Dover Publications, Inc., in 1974.

DOVER *Pictorial Archive* SERIES

Plant and Floral Woodcuts for Designers and Craftsmen belongs to the Dover Pictorial Archive Series. Up to ten illustrations may be used on any one project or in any single publication, free and without special permission. Wherever possible, include a credit line indicating the title of this book, author and publisher. Please address the publisher for permission to make more extensive use of illustrations in this book than that authorized above.
The reproduction of this book in whole is prohibited.

International Standard Book Number: 0-486-20722-6
Library of Congress Catalog Card Number: 74-77285

Manufactured in the United States of America
Dover Publications, Inc.
180 Varick Street
New York, N. Y. 10014

Publisher's Note

THE present volume offers a representative selection of botanical woodcuts from one of the masterworks in this field, the 1601 *Rariorum plantarum historia* (Account of rare plants) by Clusius, father of descriptive botany.

Charles de l'Ecluse (whose Latinized humanistic name was Carolus Clusius) was born to a noble family at Arras, capital of the Artois region in northern France, in 1524, 1525 or 1526—accounts differ. His youth was devoted to the study of law, but in the course of his extensive student travels his interests shifted to botany and medicine, and by 1555 he had become a doctor.

In 1564 he traveled through western France into Spain, where he made extensive cuttings and wrote detailed descriptions of the flora. These researches were published in his *Rariorum aliquot stirpium per Hispanias observatorum historia* (Account of some rare plants seen in Spain) of 1576. The book filled an important gap, for little attention had previously been paid to the natural history of Spain.

In 1573 Clusius accepted an invitation from Holy Roman Emperor Maximilian II to superintend the imperial gardens in Vienna. He filled the post for 14 years, continuing into the reign of Rudolph II. Weary of court life, he then withdrew to Frankfurt, where he lived in relative seclusion on a pension from the Landgrave of Hesse. In 1589 Clusius moved to Leyden to occupy the chair of botany at the university, a post which he held until his death in 1609.

Clusius either knew personally or corresponded with many of the scholars of the age, including such leading botanists as Dodonaeus (Rembert Dodoens), Matthias de Lobel and the Englishman John Gerard, superintendent of Lord Burghley's gardens and author of the famous *Herball* (1597). Gerard gave Clusius samples of the potato, a plant that Sir Francis Drake had brought back from Peru. After successfully growing potatoes in Leyden, Clusius, in turn, sent some of these plants on to colleagues in Italy. The yellow rose was also introduced to Europe by Clusius from the Balkans and Persia; and, by planting tulips (which had come from Constantinople and the Levant) in Leyden, Clusius was partly responsible for the establishment of the tulip trade in Holland and the "tulipomania" that swept that country in the seventeenth century.

In 1601 the *Rariorum plantarum historia*, Clusius' chief work, was published in Antwerp. It was printed under the direction of Johannes Moretus (Moerentorf) at the famous house of Plantin, which specialized in botanical books and also published works by Dodonaeus and Lobel. The text is evidence of Clusius' learning. Not only does he list plants by their Latin names, but he is also able to give the names by which they were commonly known in several languages. He describes the medicinal properties of various plants, and cites ancient authors such as Pliny. Moreover, his descriptions have great accuracy and elegance.

Some of the woodcuts that appear in the *Rariorum plantarum historia* had originally been used in earlier works. Several came from books by Clusius himself which had been published by Plantin in 1576 and 1583. These blocks had been designed by Pieter van der Borcht the Elder and had been cut by Jansen van Kampen and A. Nicolai. Designs for other cuts in the *Rariorum plantarum historia* have been attributed to Virgil Solis the Younger.

There are certainly other sources for the woodcuts in the *Rariorum plantarum historia*, for at this time botanists lent, borrowed, copied and stole blocks from each other as a matter of course. Many of the woodcuts that appear in the *Rariorum plantarum historia* were later incorporated by Thomas Johnson into his 1633 edition of Gerard's *Herball*.

The fine engraved title page of the *Rariorum plantarum historia*, reproduced as the frontispiece to the present work, has been attributed to the noted printmaker Jakob de Gheyn. De Gheyn also executed a portrait of Clusius to appear in the volume but, although a poem about the portrait was part of the book, the portrait was not included.

Of the more than 1,000 woodcuts that appeared in Clusius' masterwork, 419 are reproduced here. This selection contains many of the most artistically successful and also reflects the scope and variety of the original work.

The Latin names by which Clusius identifies the plants (these names do not follow modern nomenclature) are listed on p. 181.

I

1

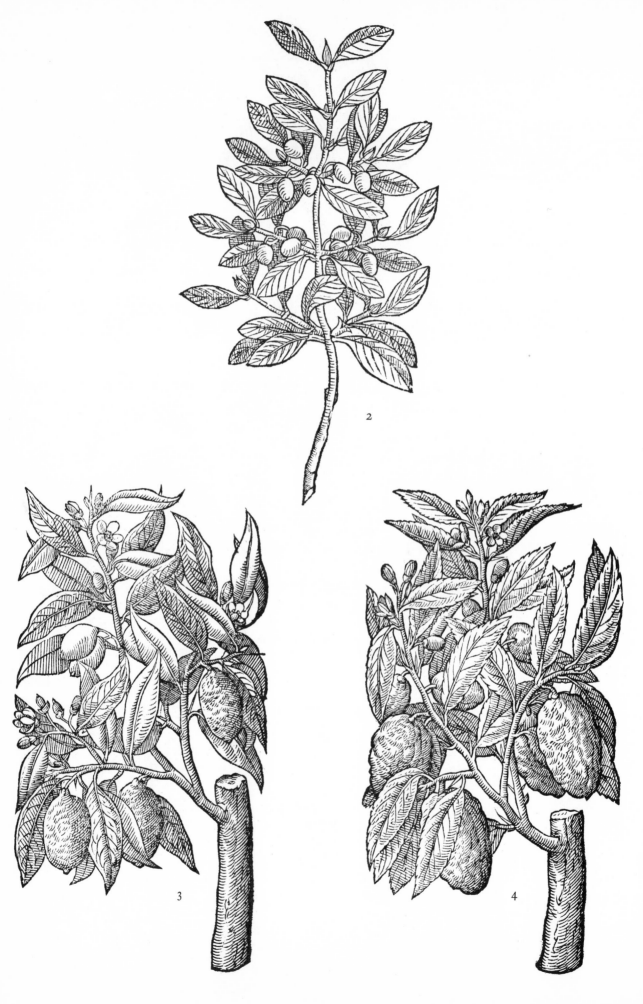

2

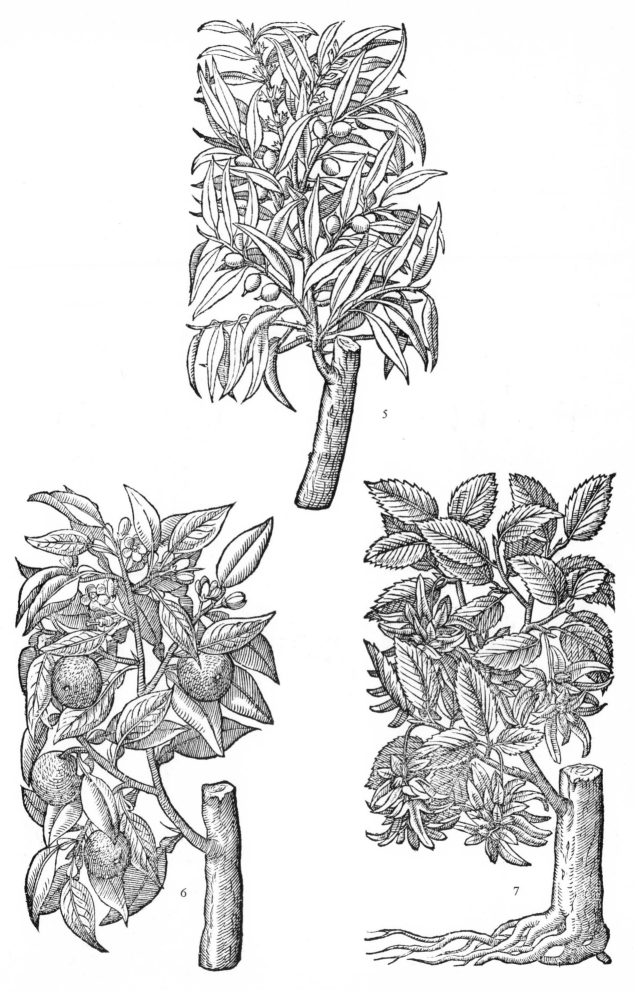

5

6

7

3

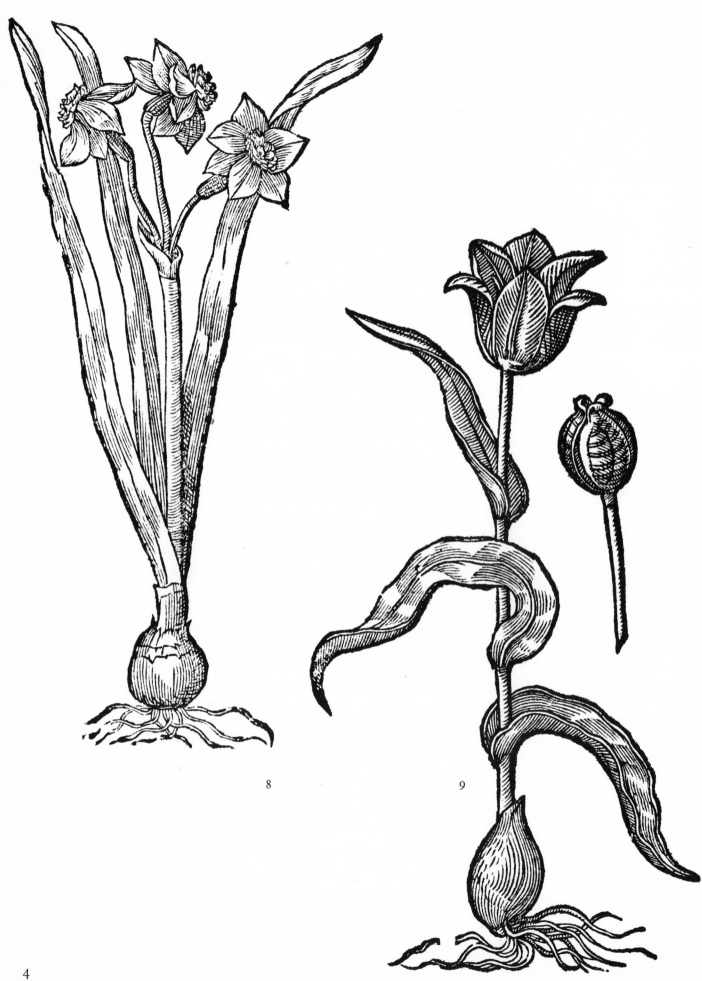

4   8   9

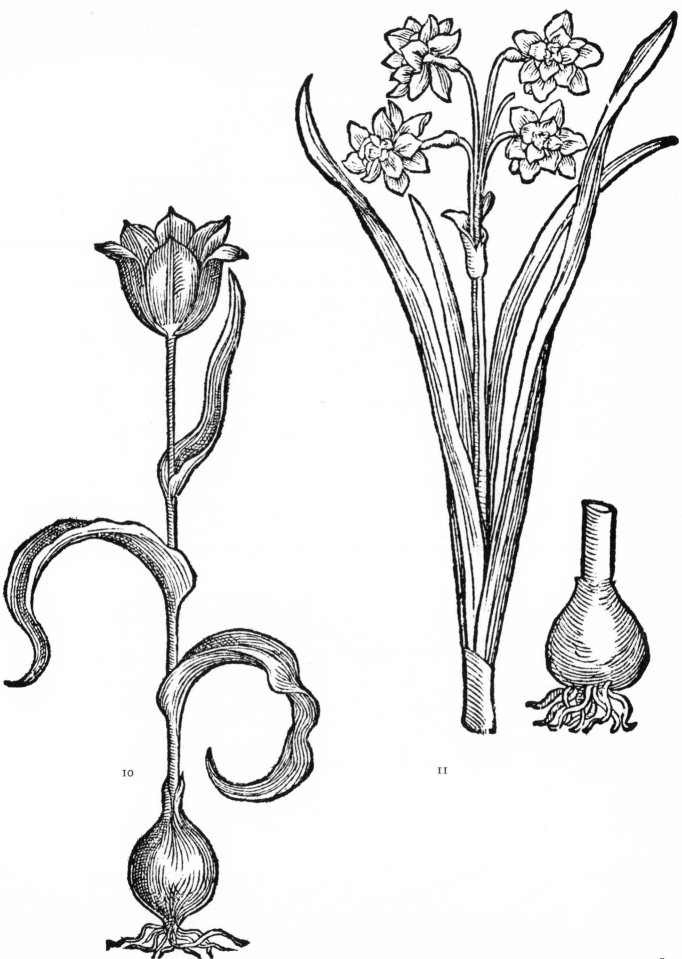

10

11

5

12

13

14

15

16

17

18   19

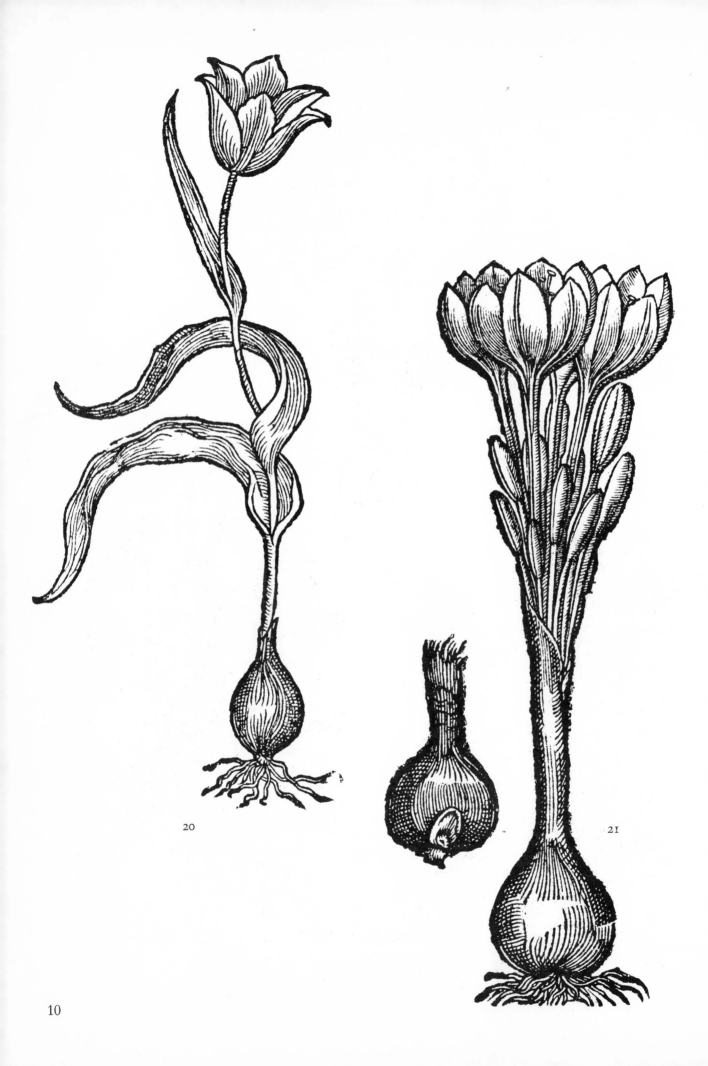

20

21

22

23

24

25

13

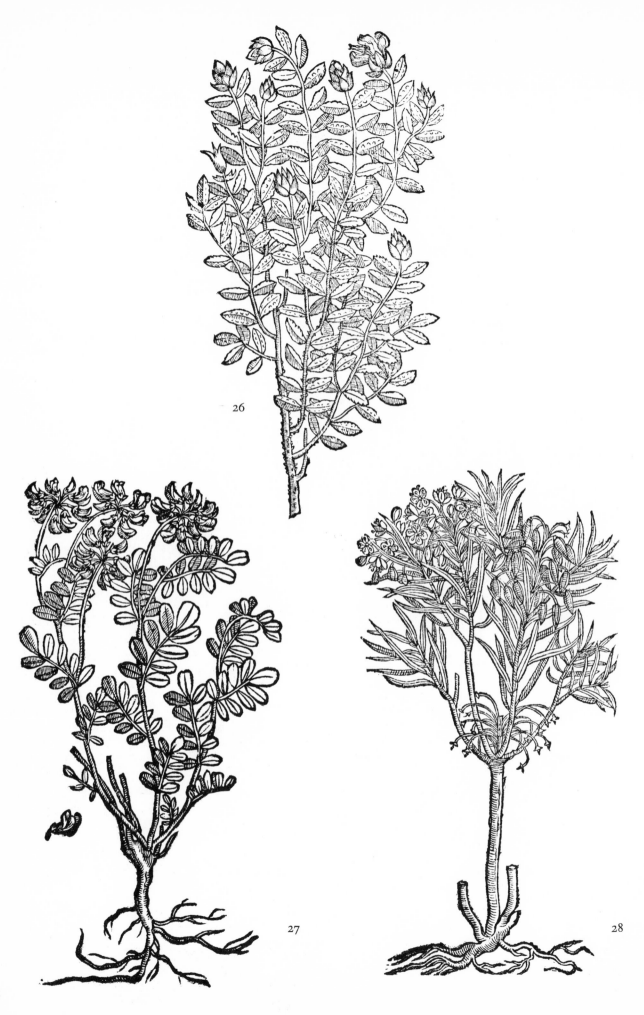

26

27

28

14

29

30

31

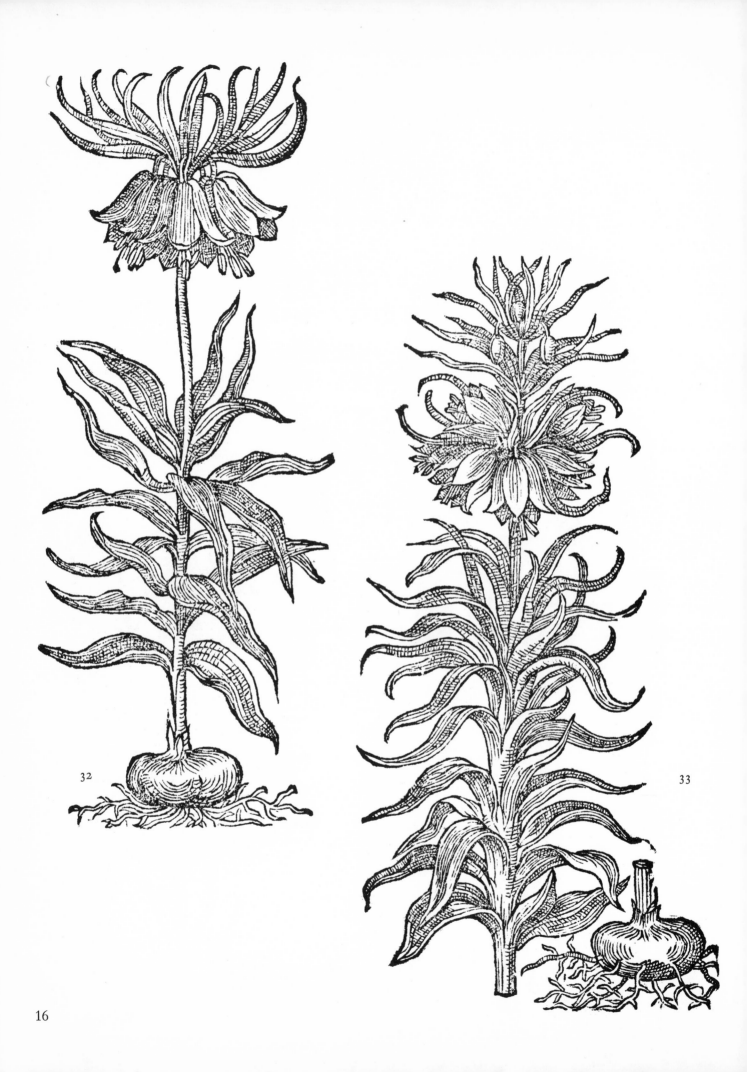

32

33

34

35

36

37

38

39

40

41

42   43

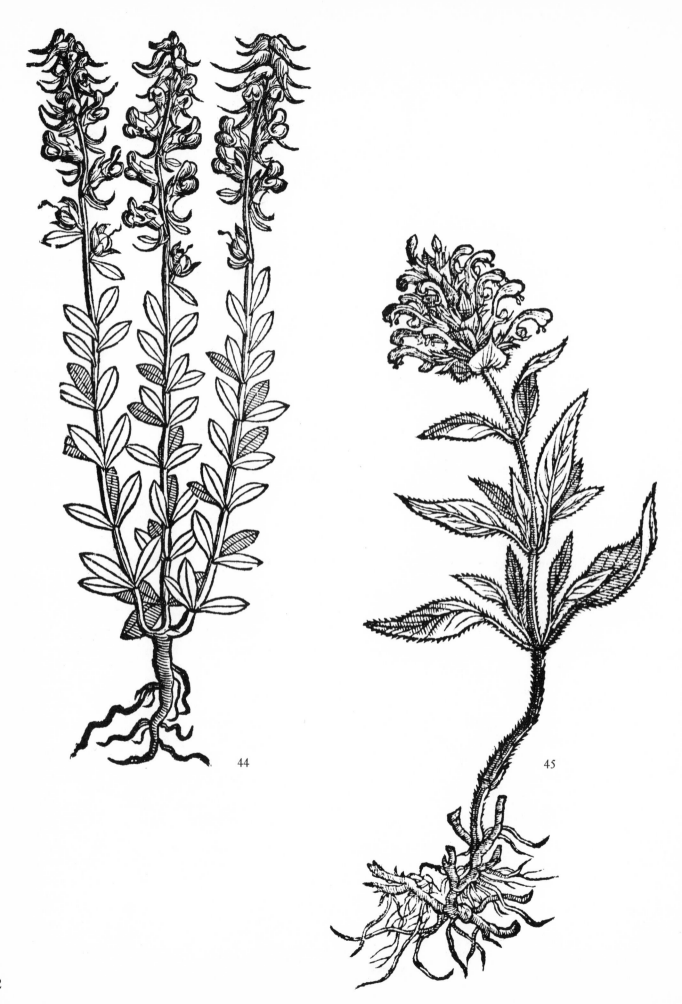

44 45

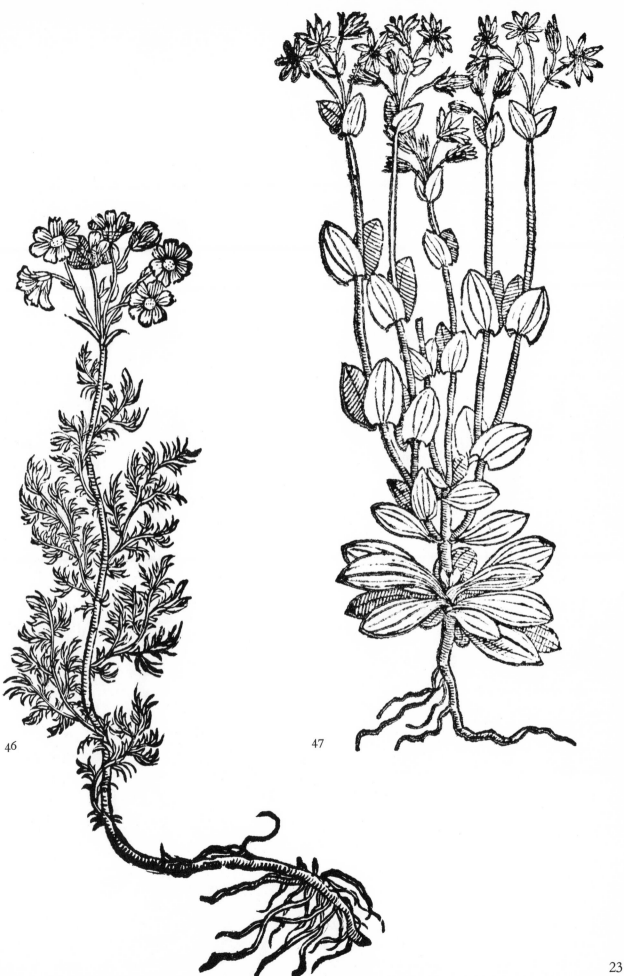

46

47

23

48

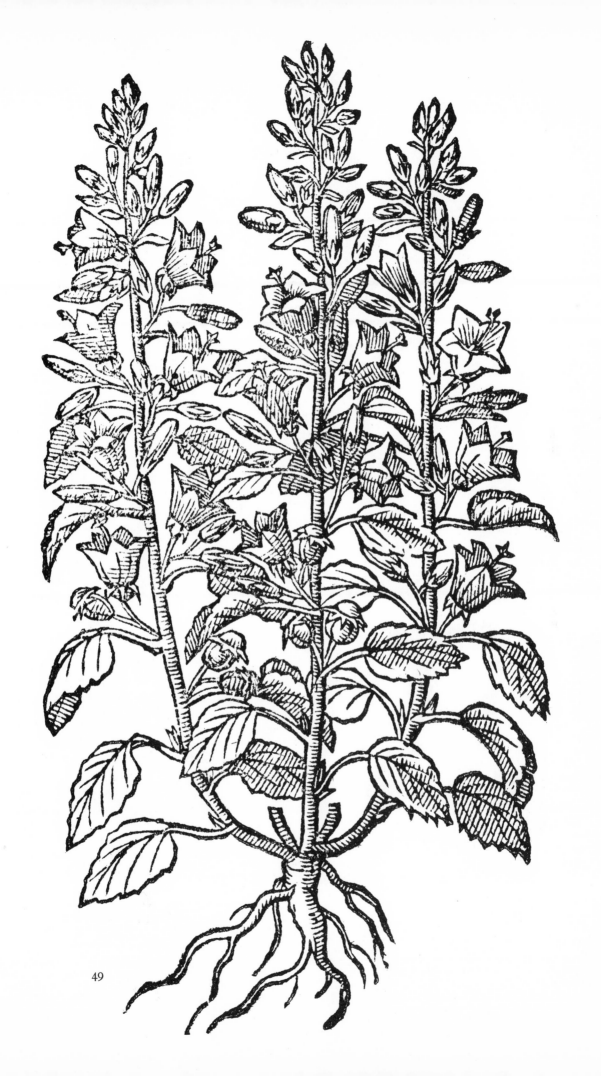

49

50

51

52

53

54

55

56

57

58

59

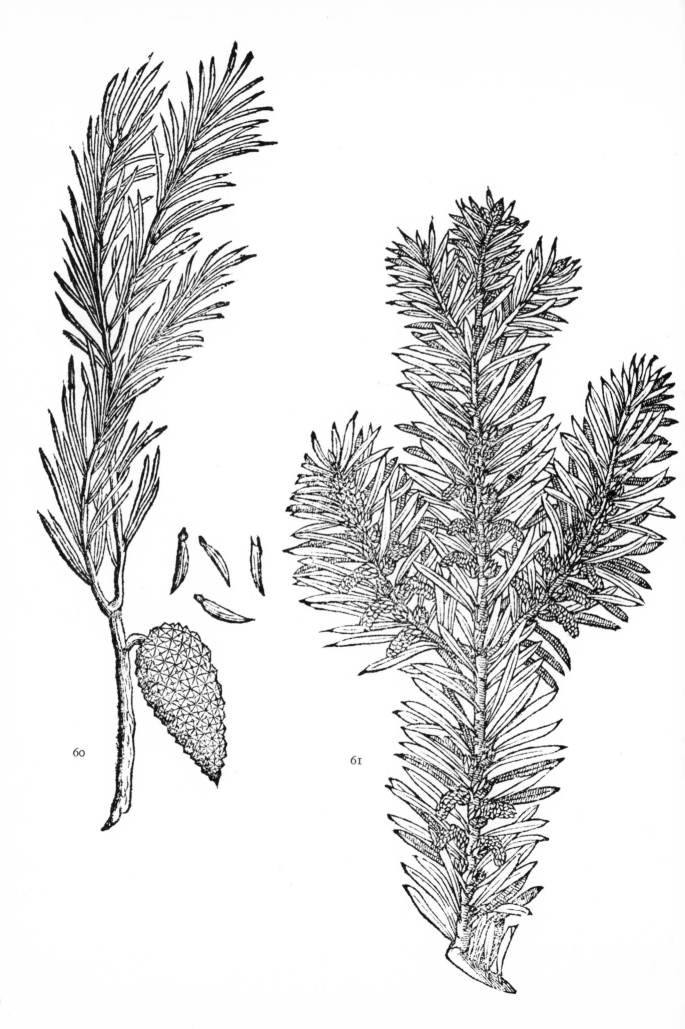

60

61

62

63

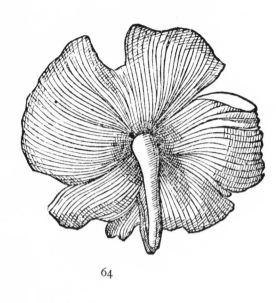

64

65

66

67

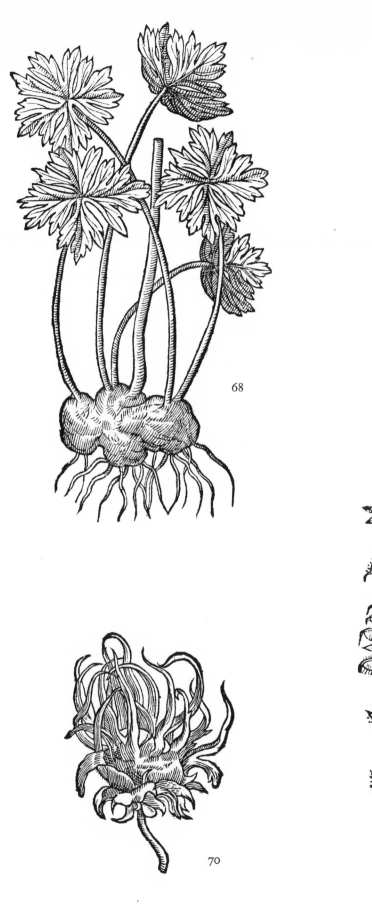

68

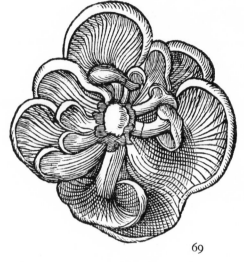

69

70

71

33

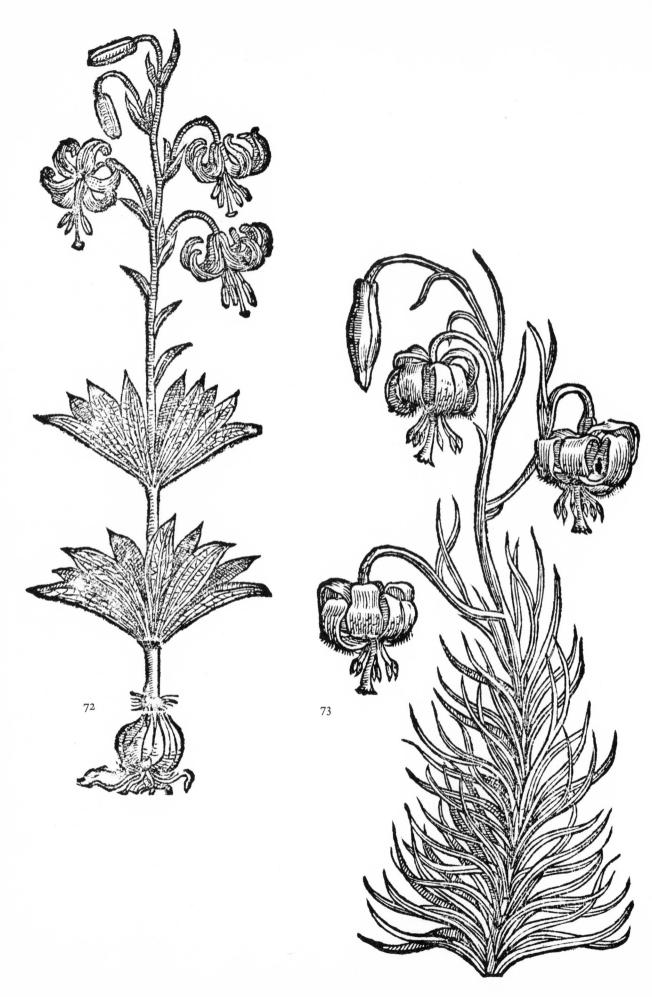

72 73

74

75

76

77

78

36

79

80

81

82

83

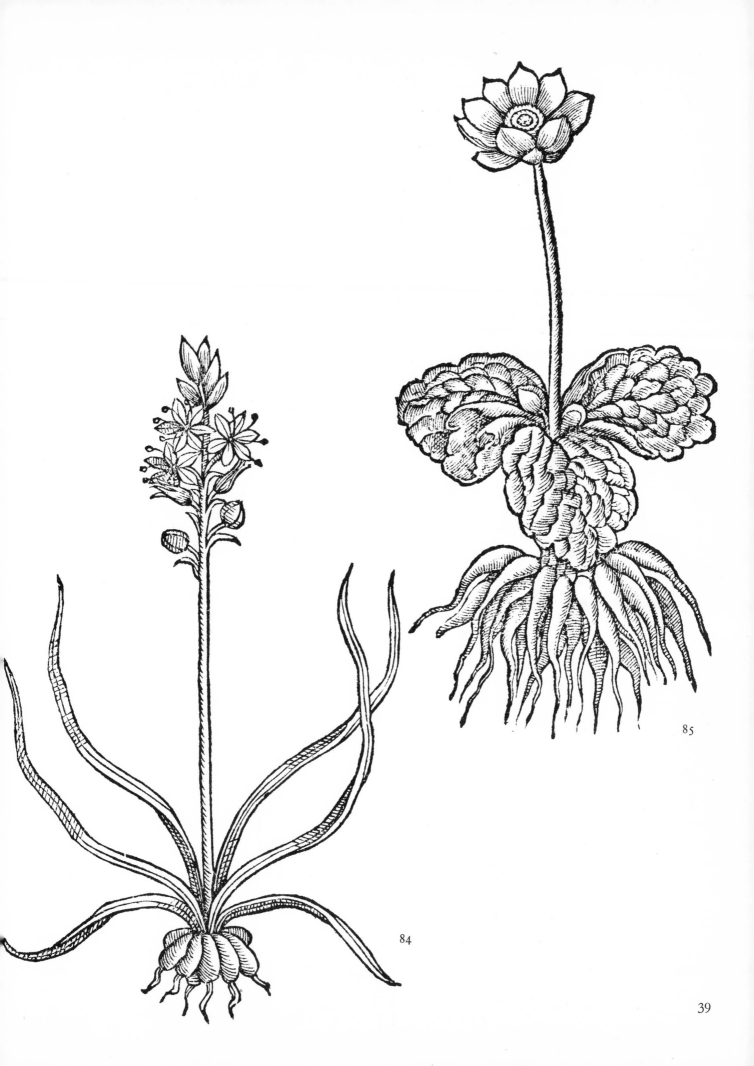

84

85

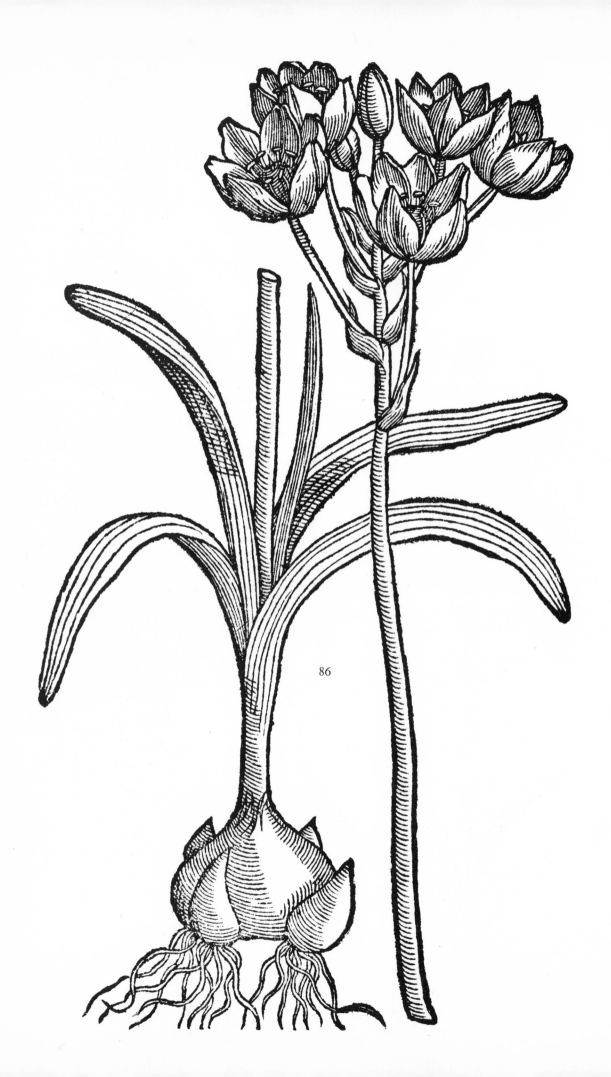

86

87

88

89

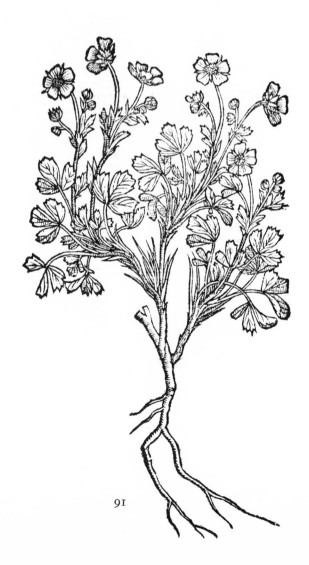

90

91

92

93   94

95

96

44

97

98

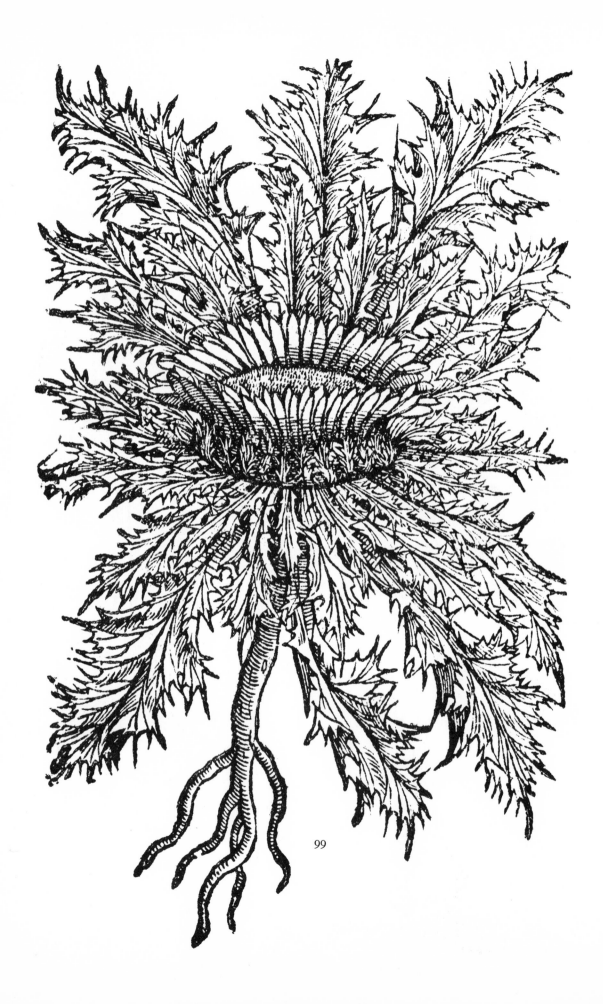

99

46

100   101

102

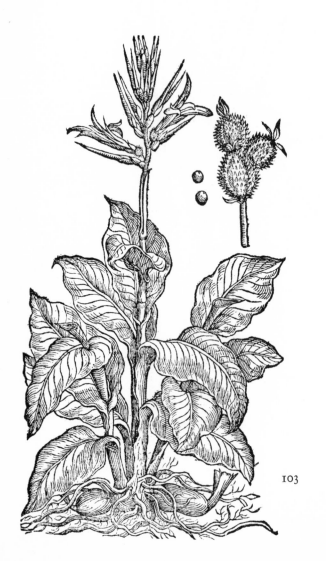

103

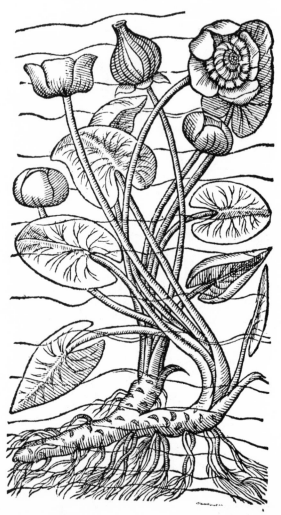

104

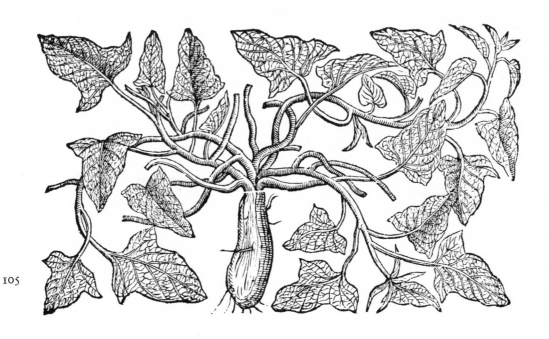

105

106

107

108

109

110

III

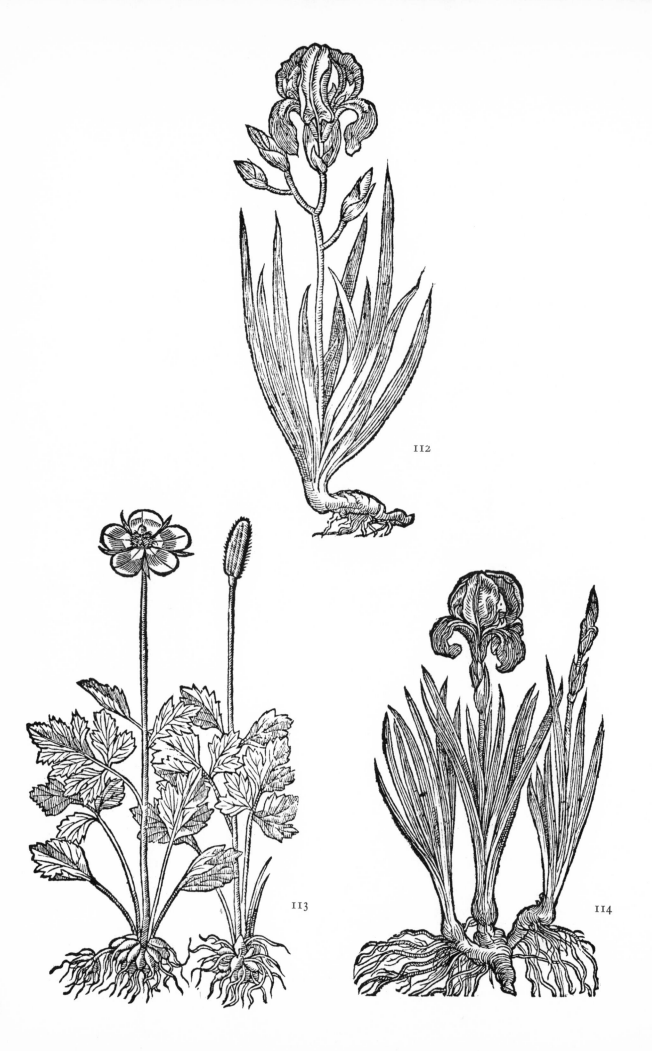

112

113

114

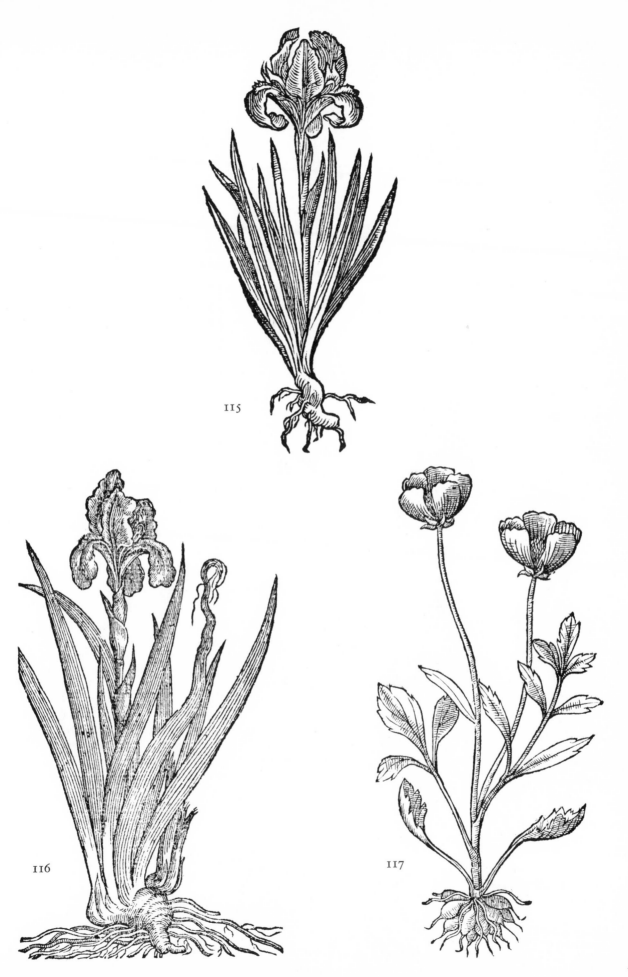

115

116

117

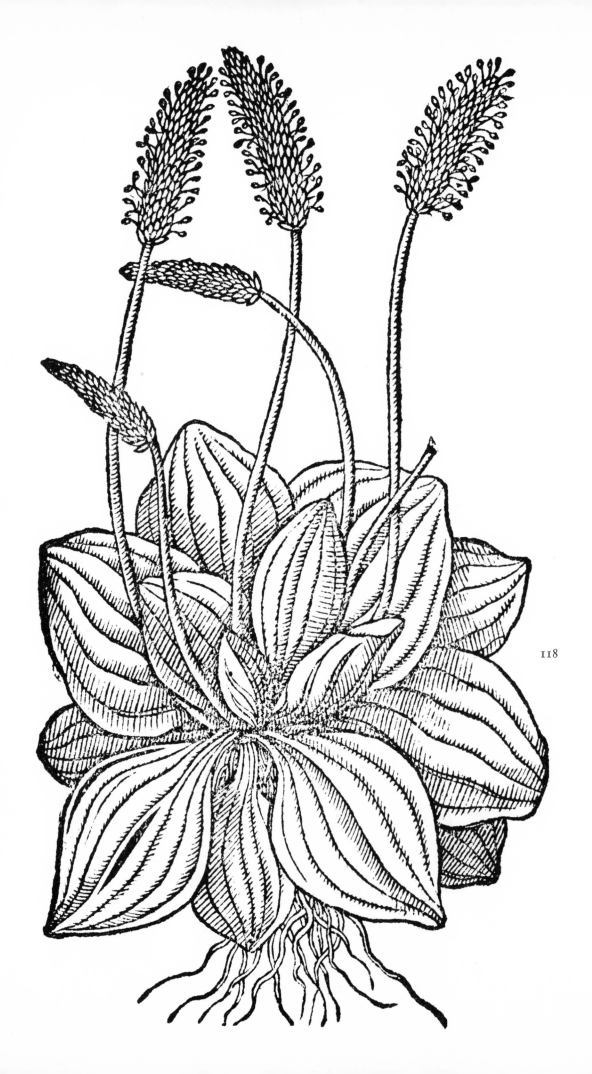

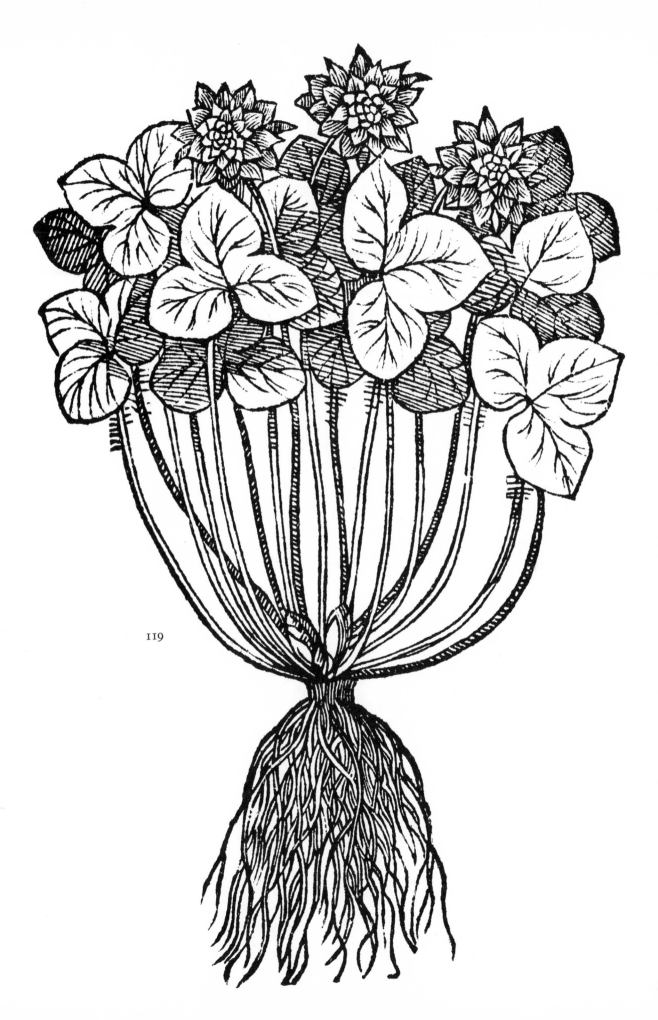

119

120

121

122

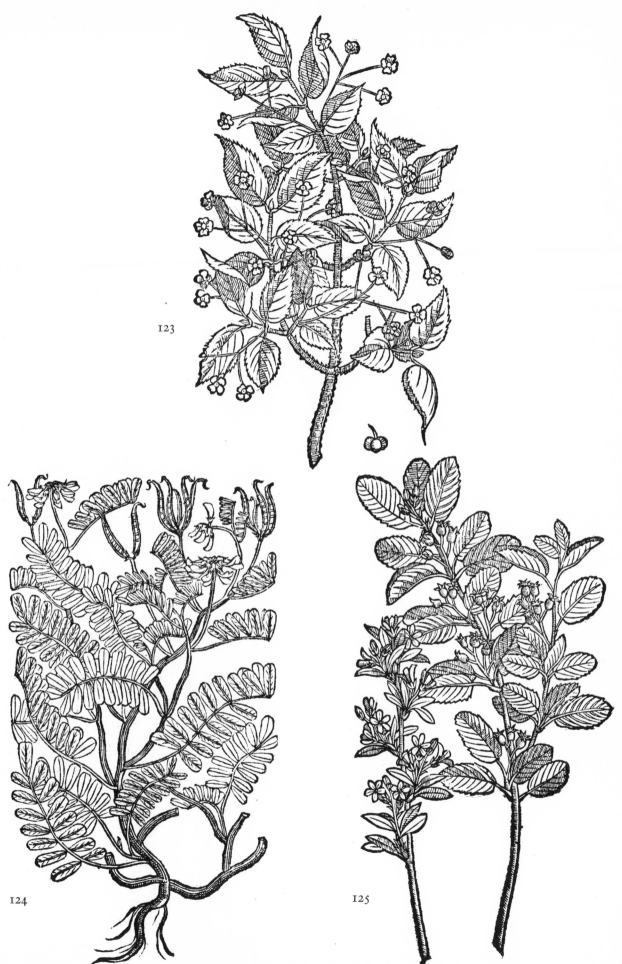

123

124   125

126

127

128

129

130

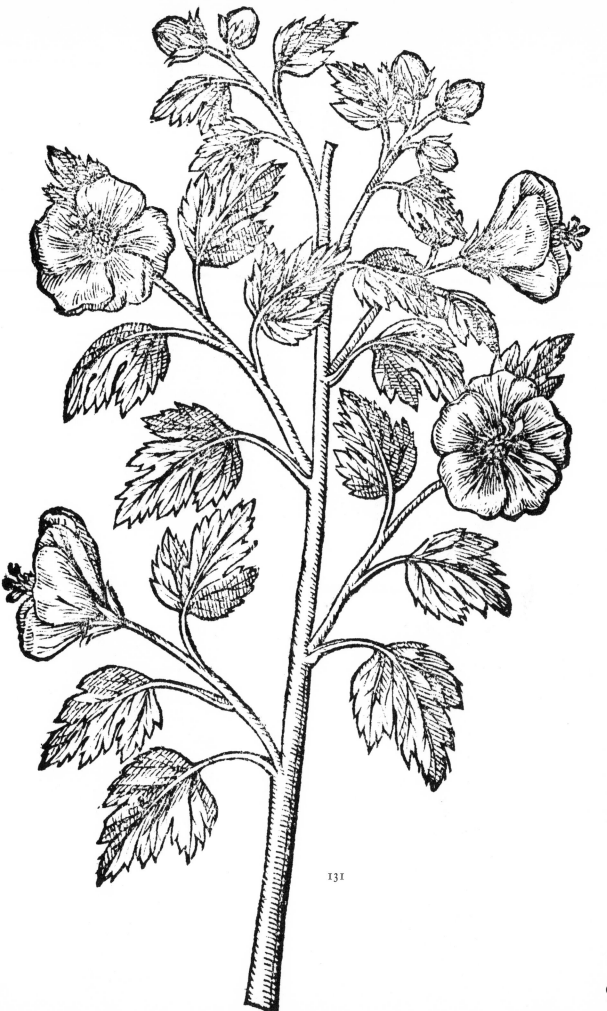

131

132

133

134

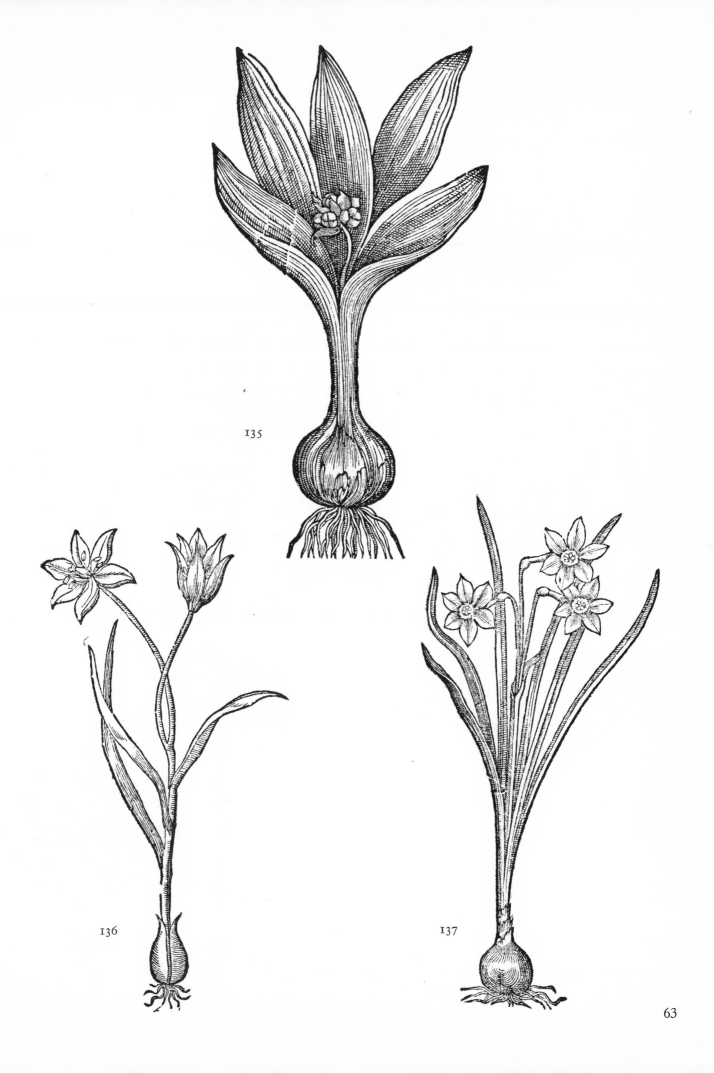

135

136

137

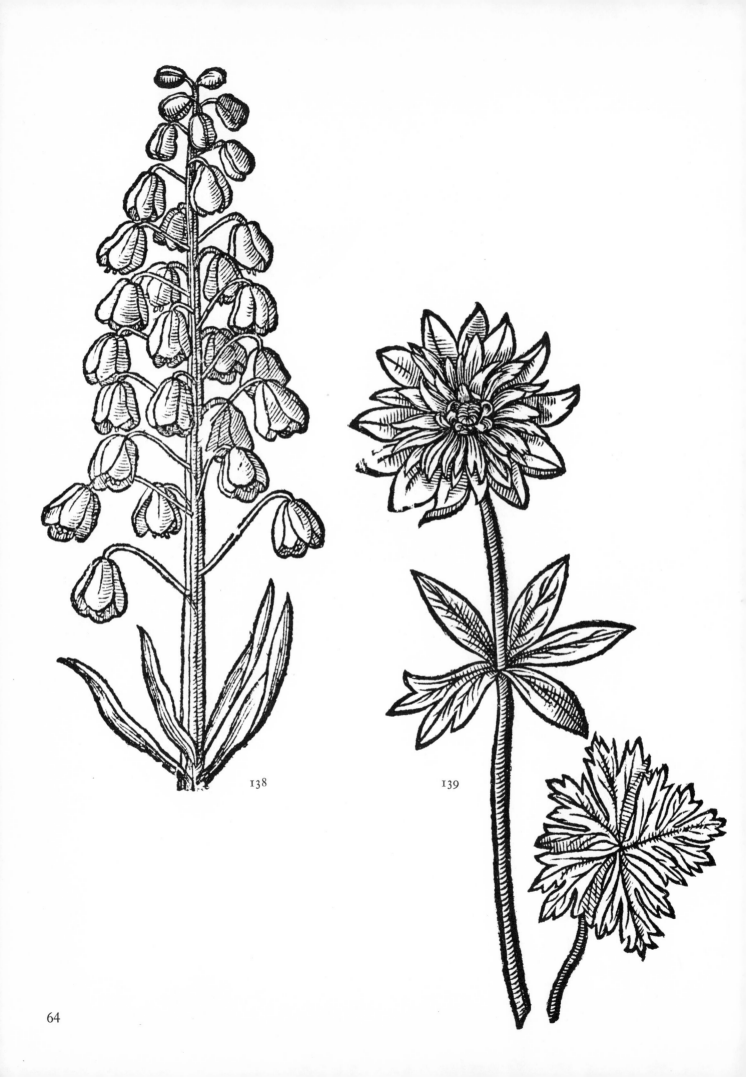

138

139

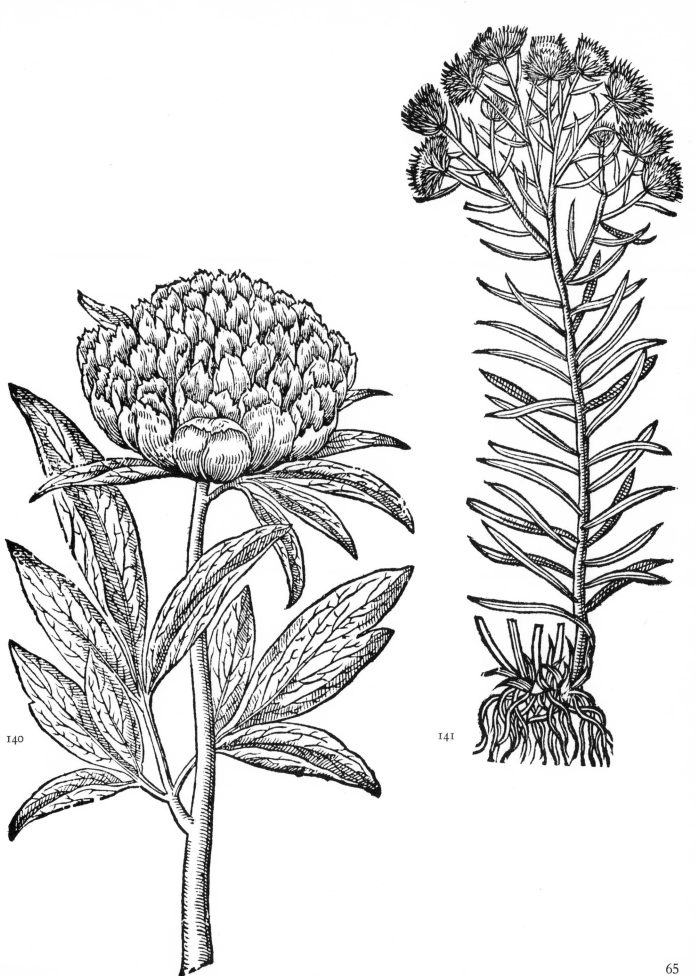

140

141

142

143

144

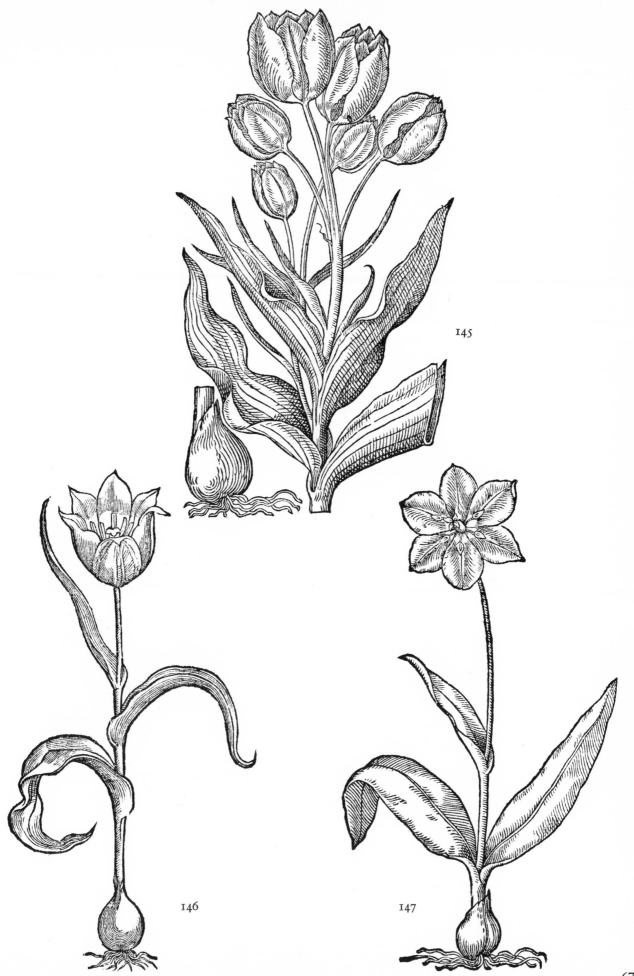

145

146   147

148

149

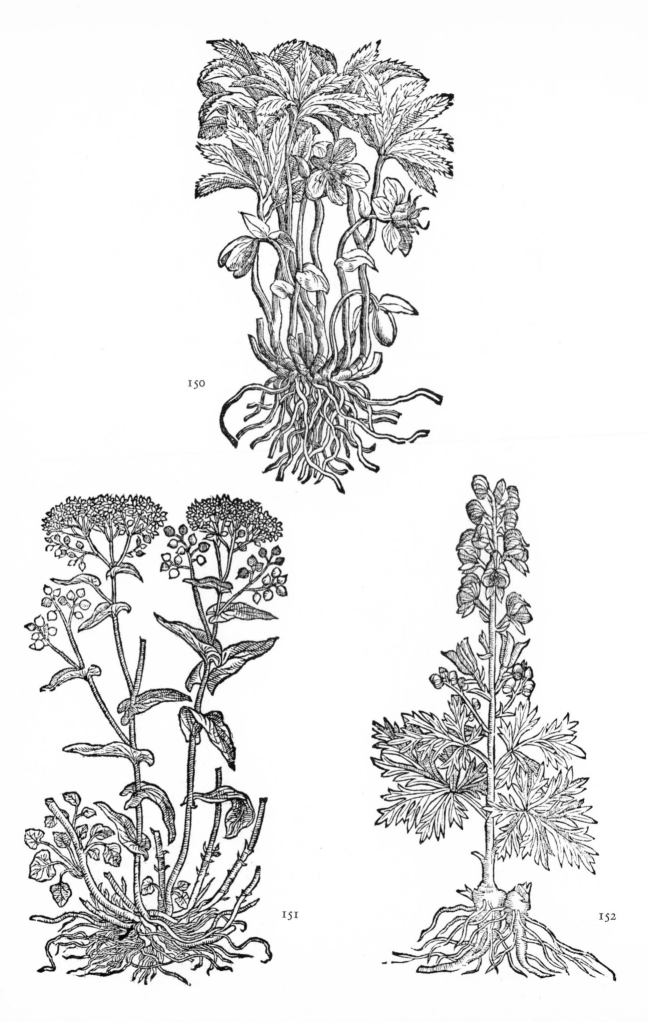

150

151

152

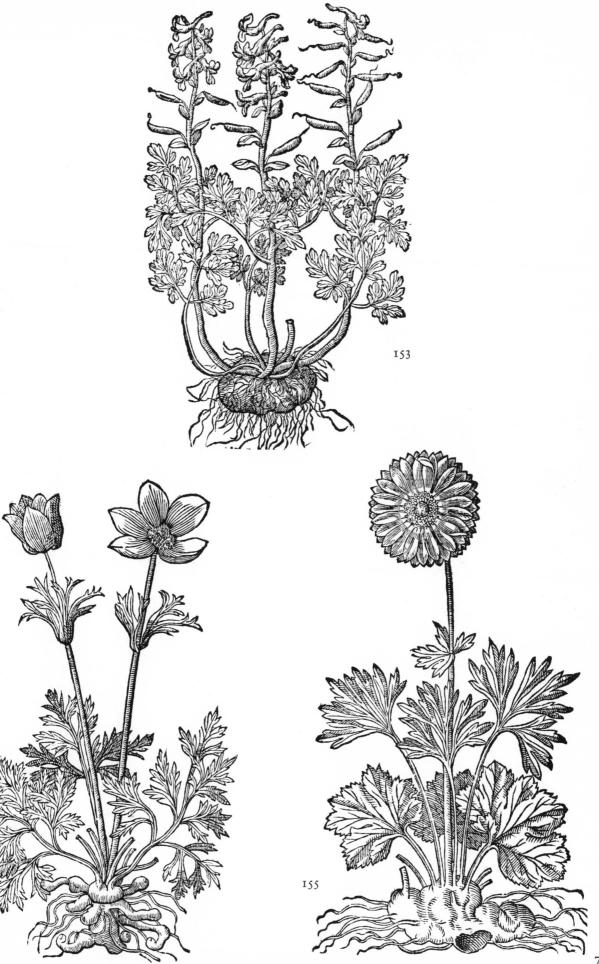

153

154   155

156   157

158

159

160

161   162

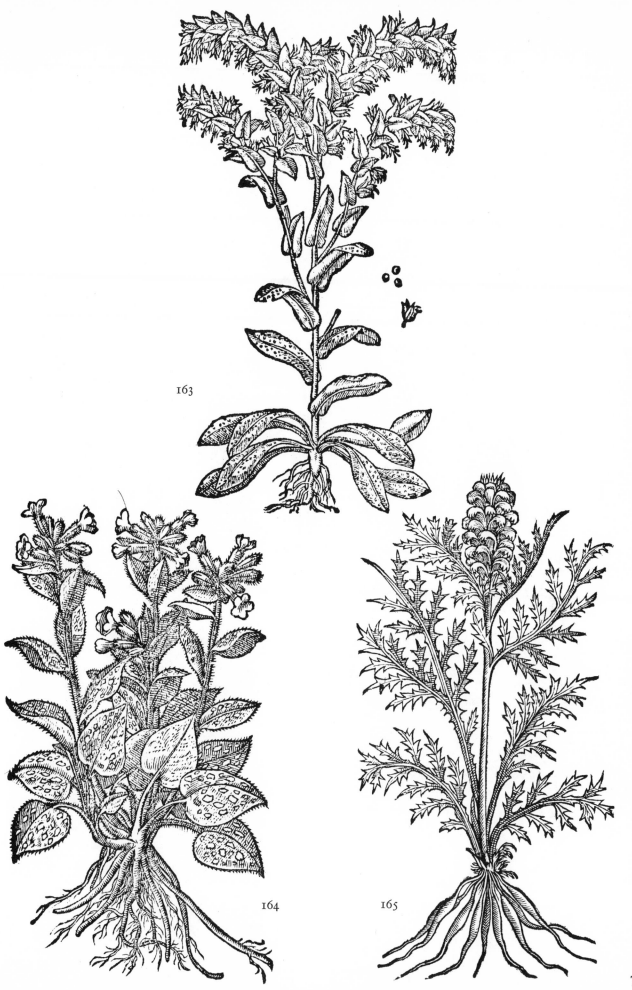

163

164   165

166

168

169

170

171

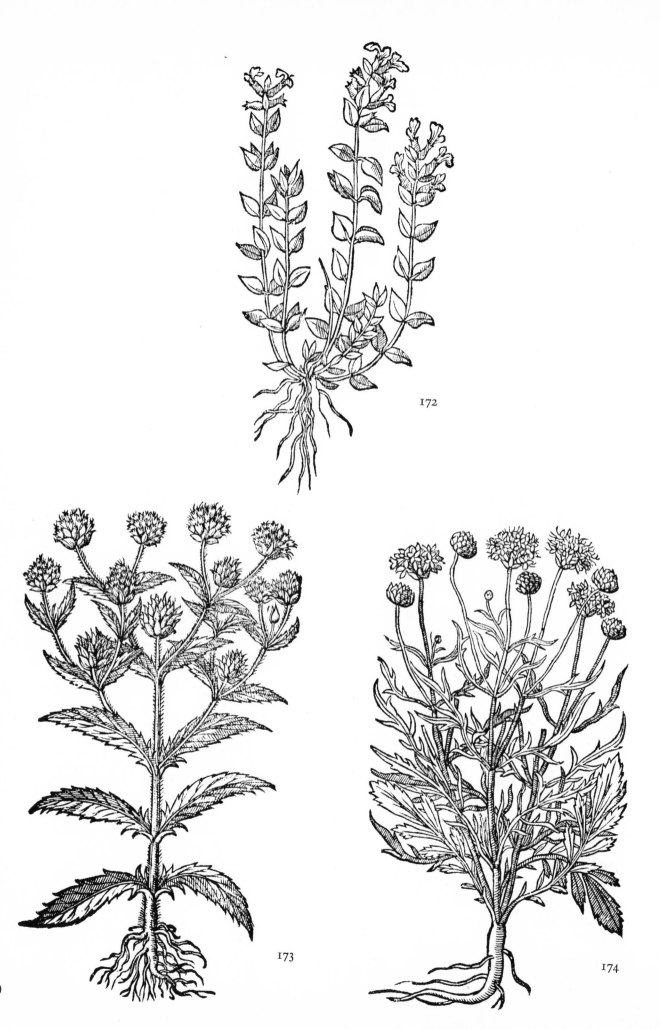

172

173

174

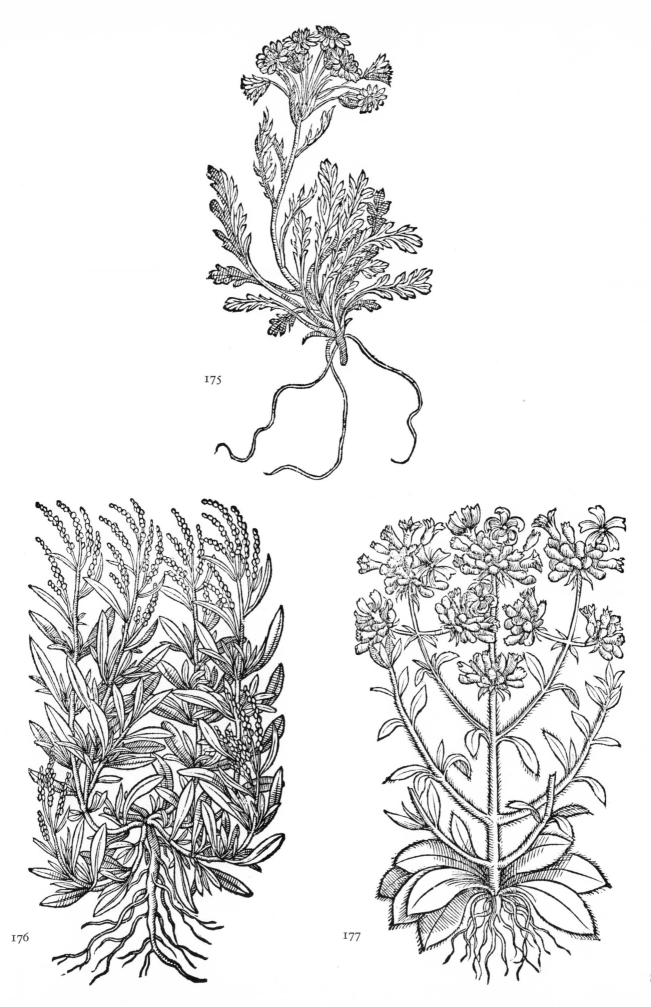

175

176   177

178

179

180   181

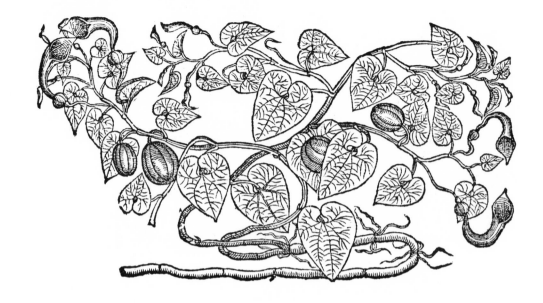

182

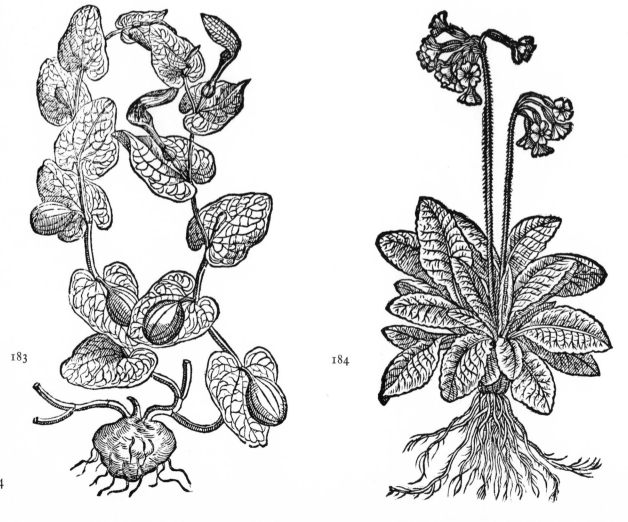

183

184

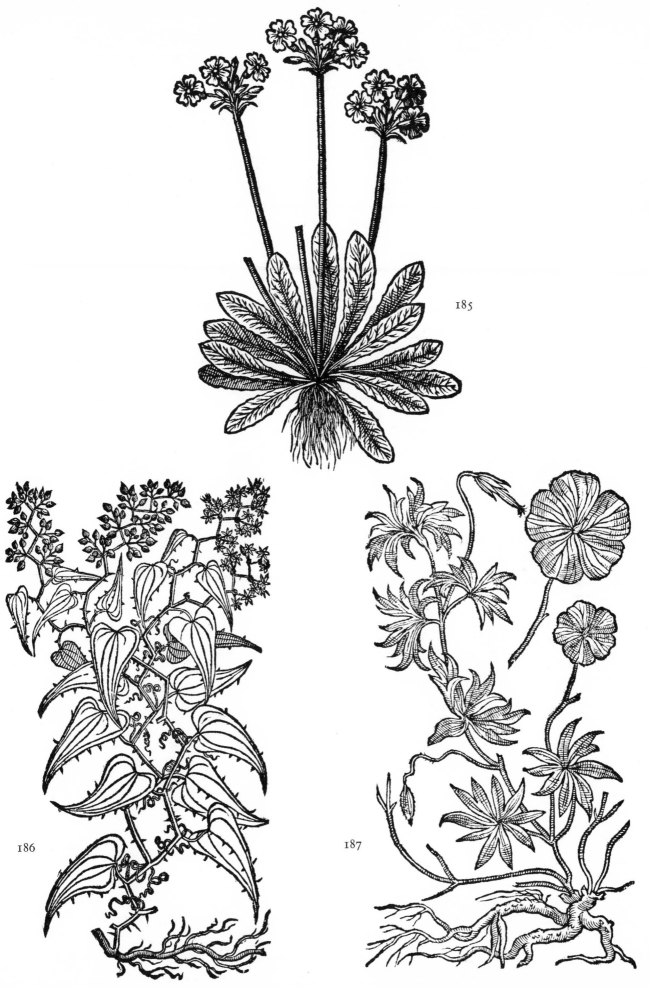

185

186   187

188

189

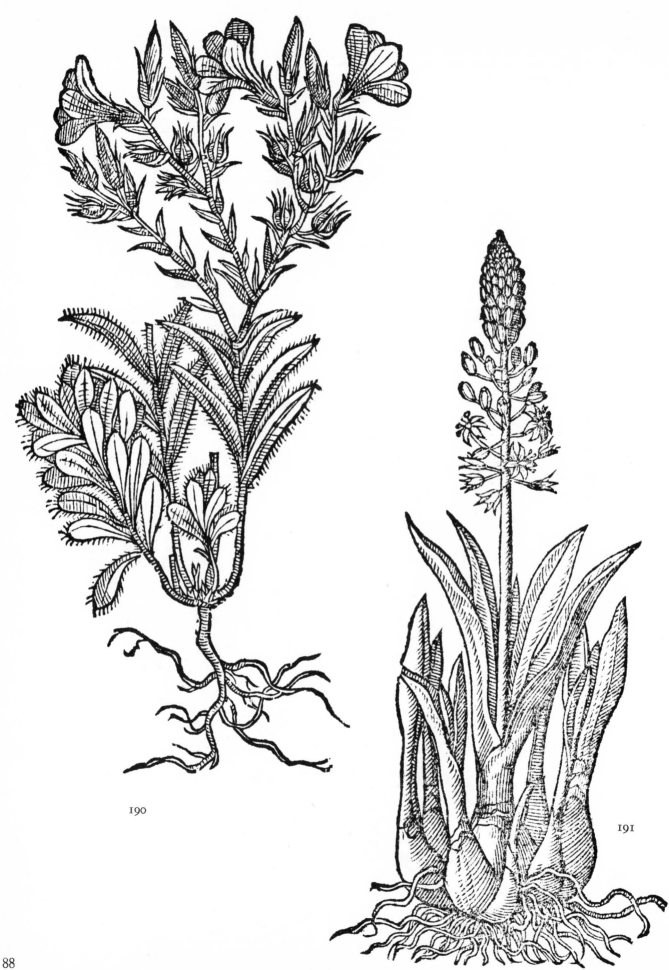

190

191

192

193

194

195

196

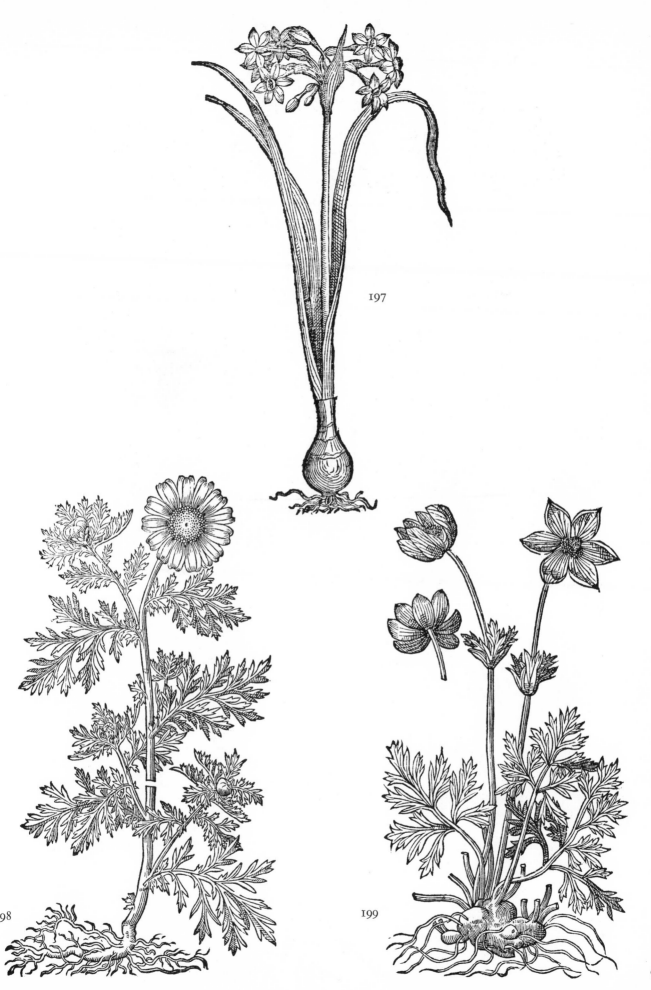

197

198

199

200

201

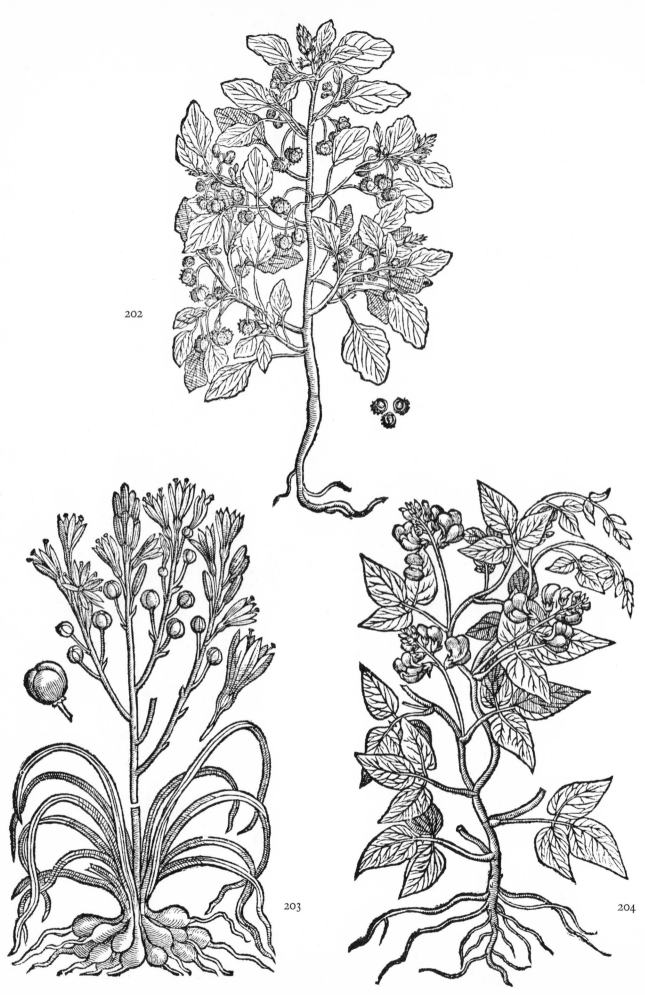

202

203

204

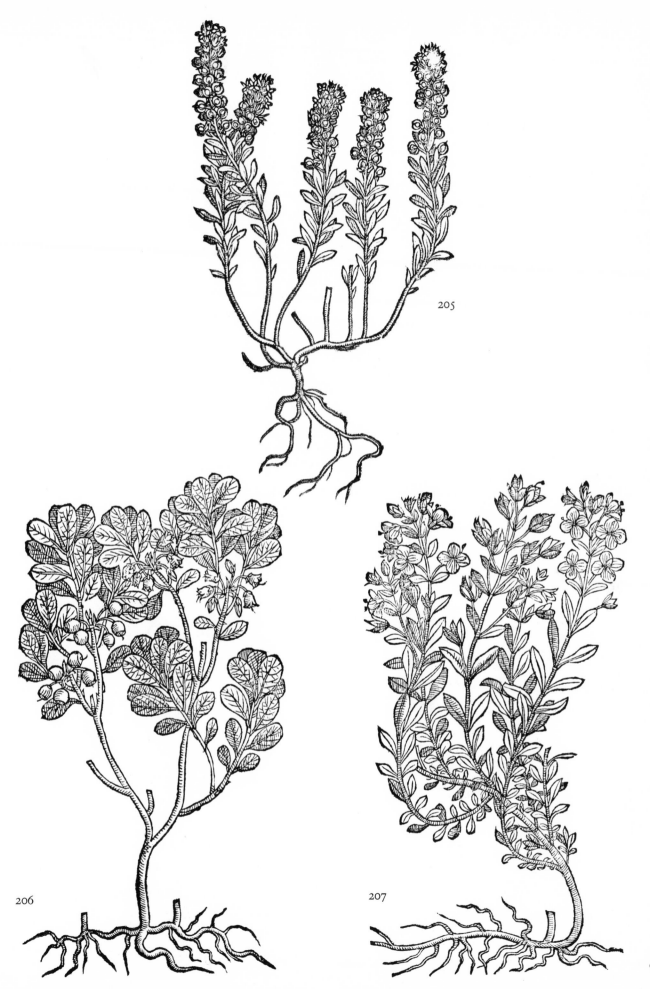

205

206

207

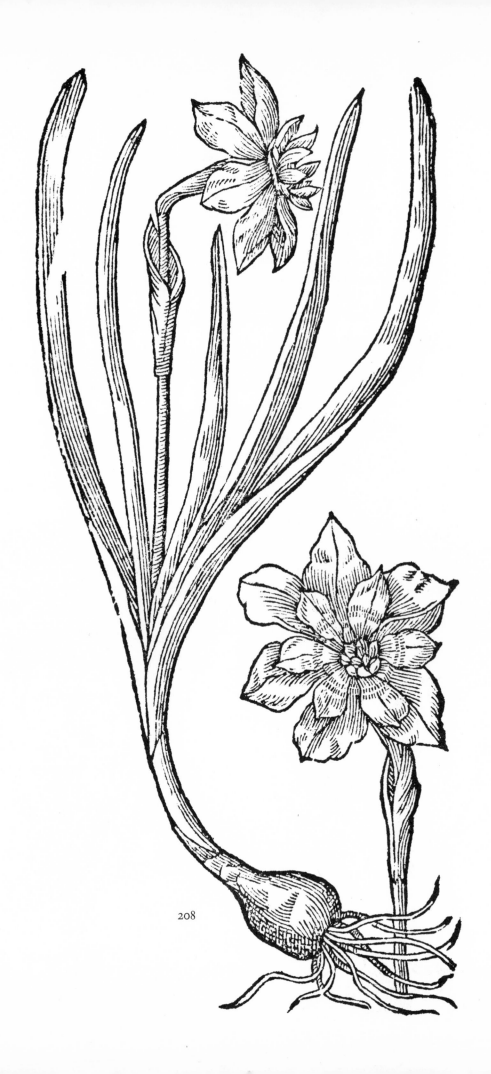

208

96

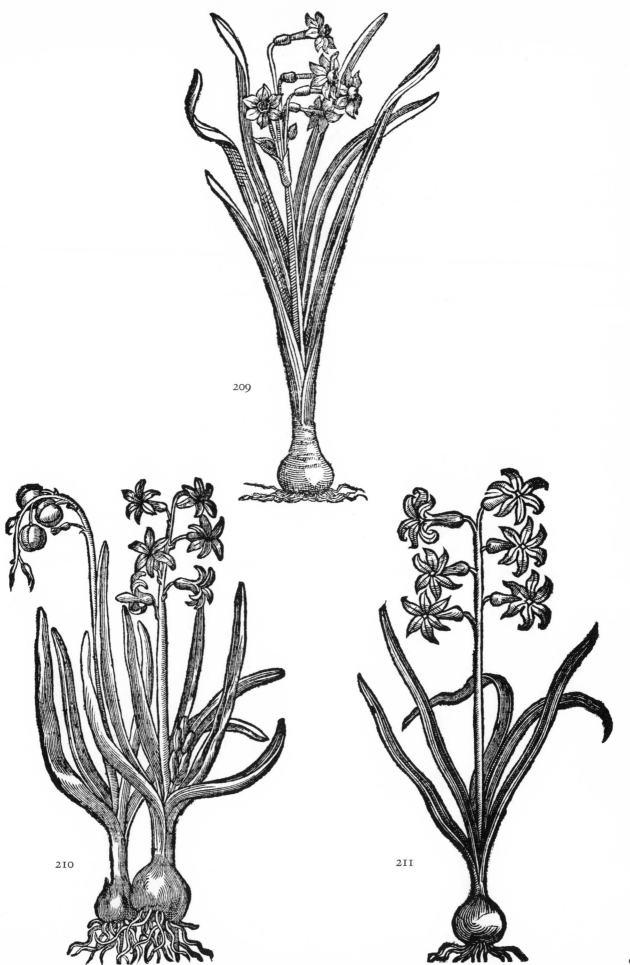

209

210

211

212

213

214

215

216   217

218

219

220

100

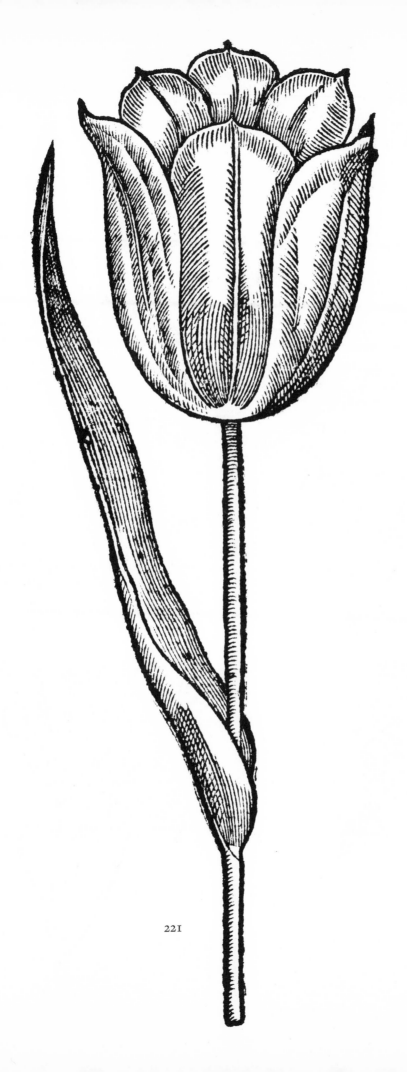

221

222   223

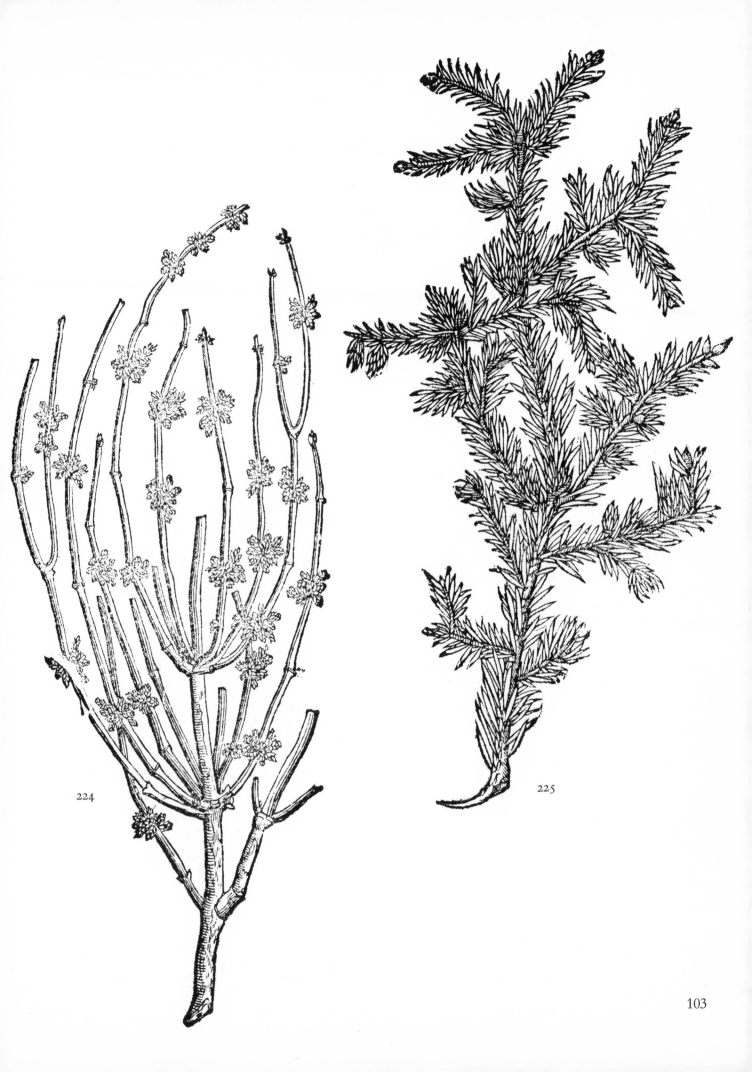

224

225

226

227   228

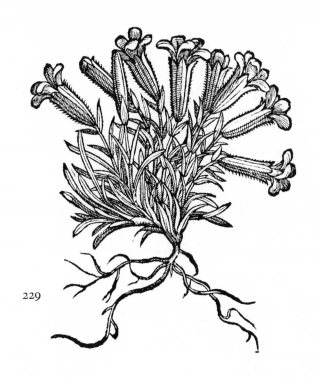

229

230   231

232

233

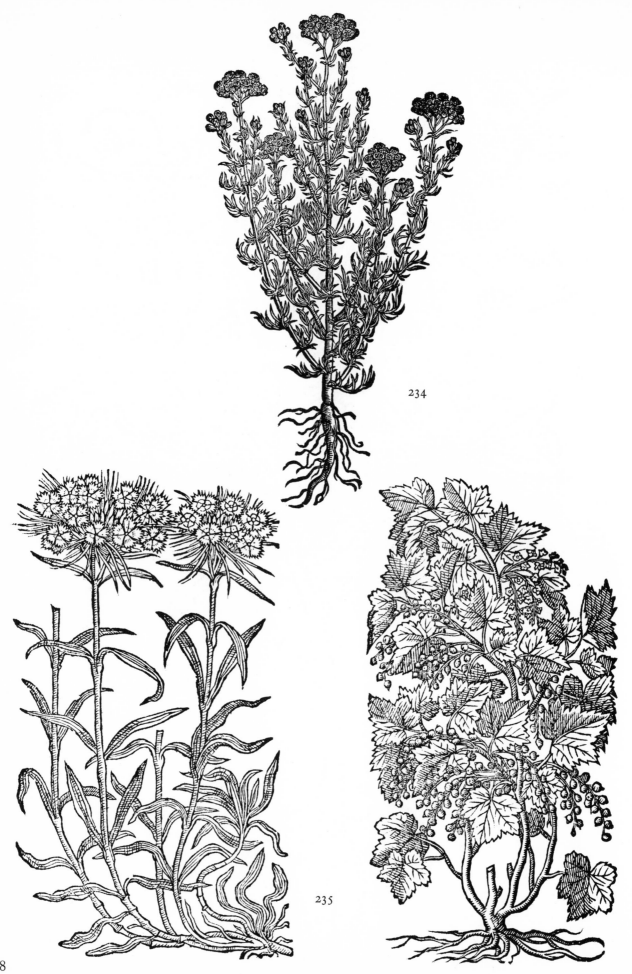

234

235

236

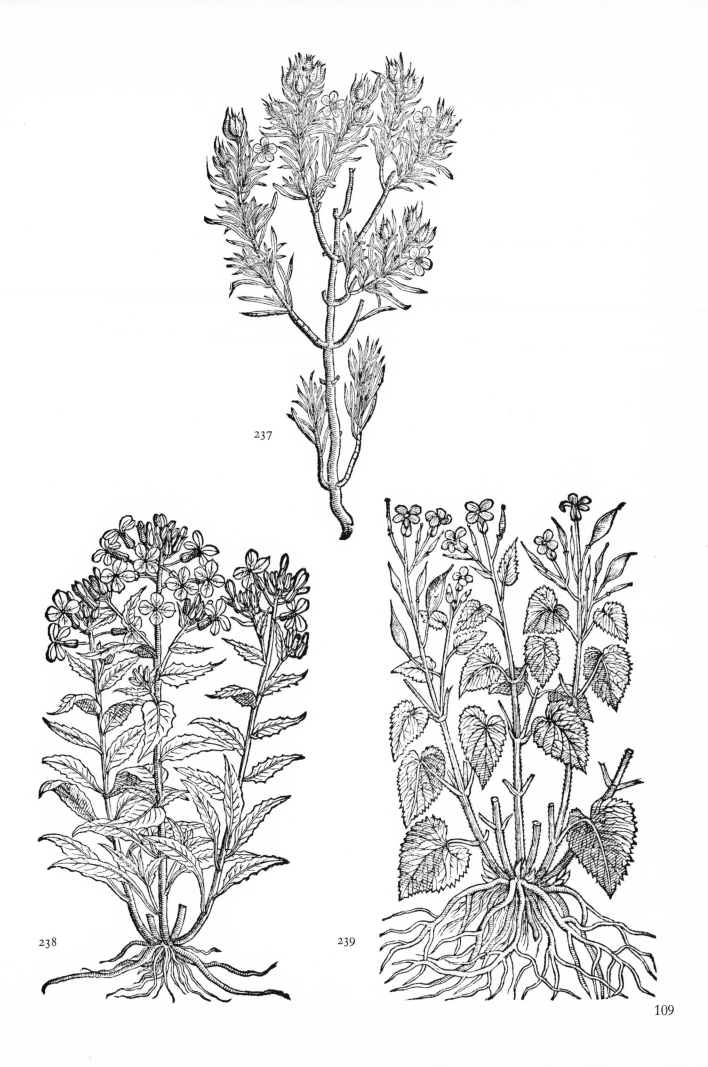

237

238   239

240   241

242

243

111

244

245

246

247

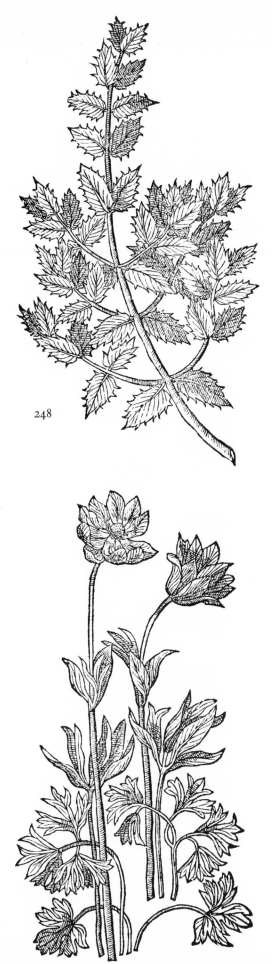

248

250

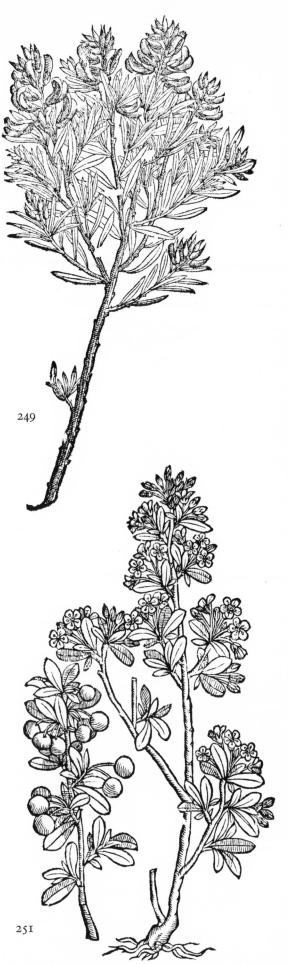

249

251

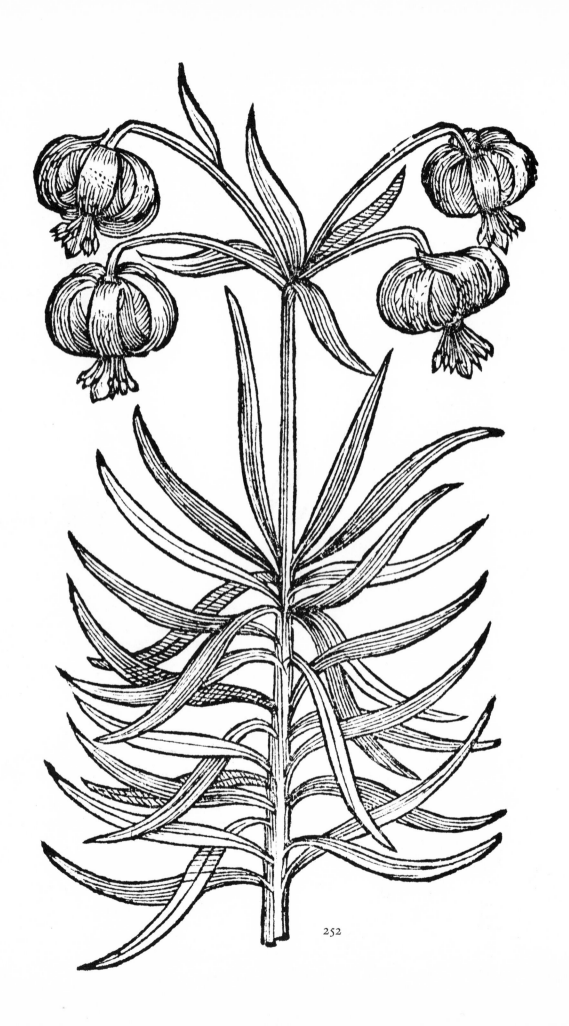

252

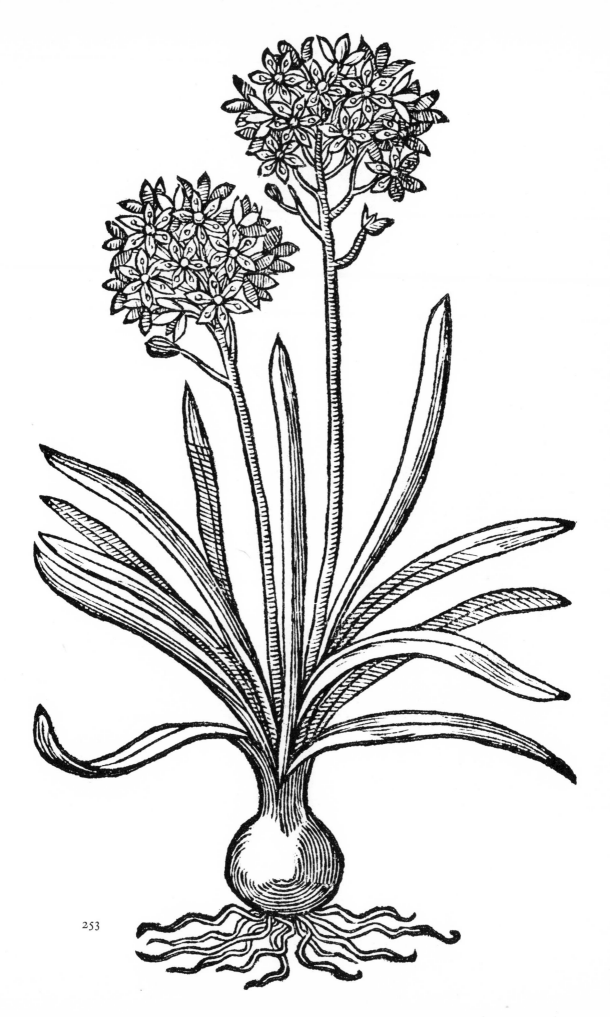

253

254

255

256

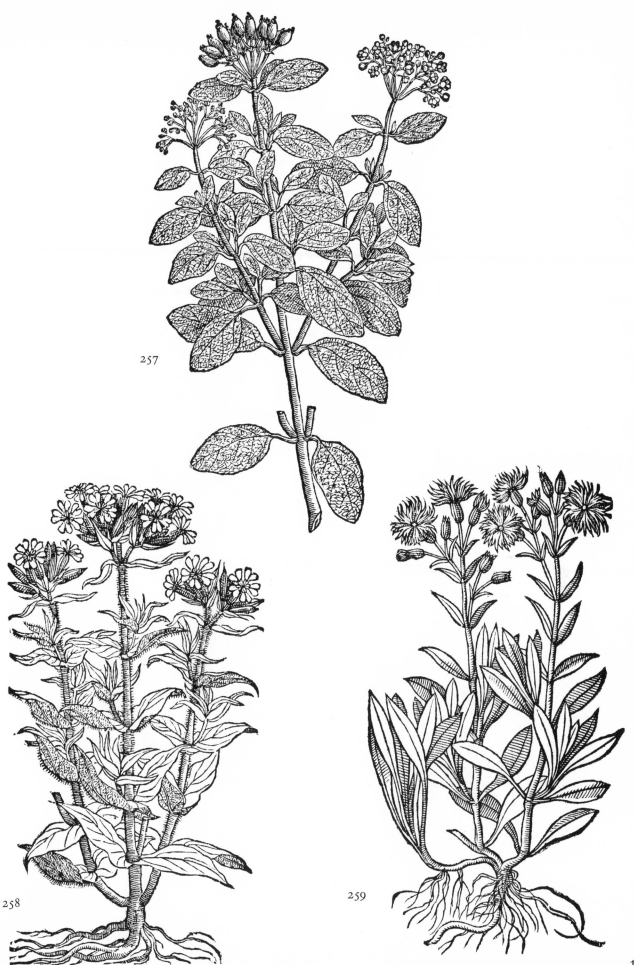

257

258

259

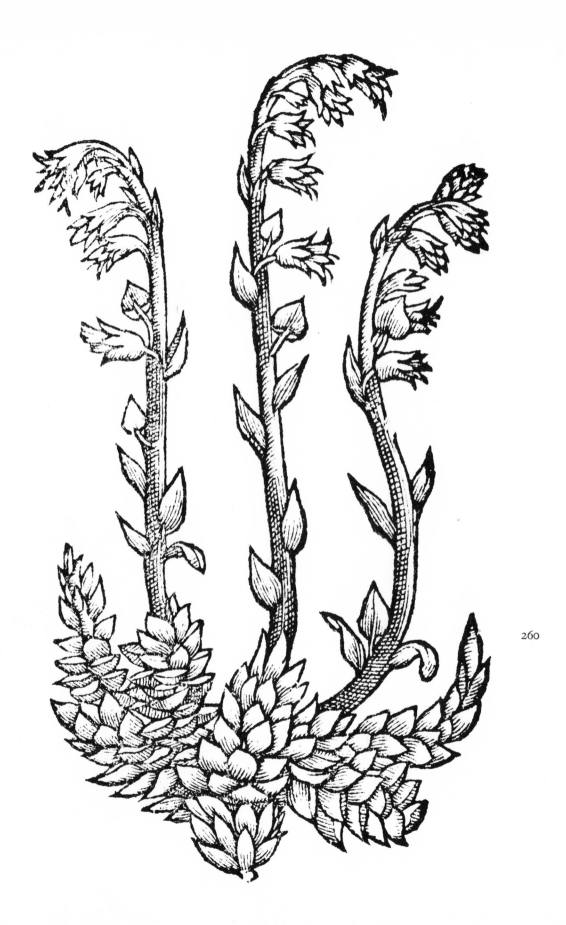

260

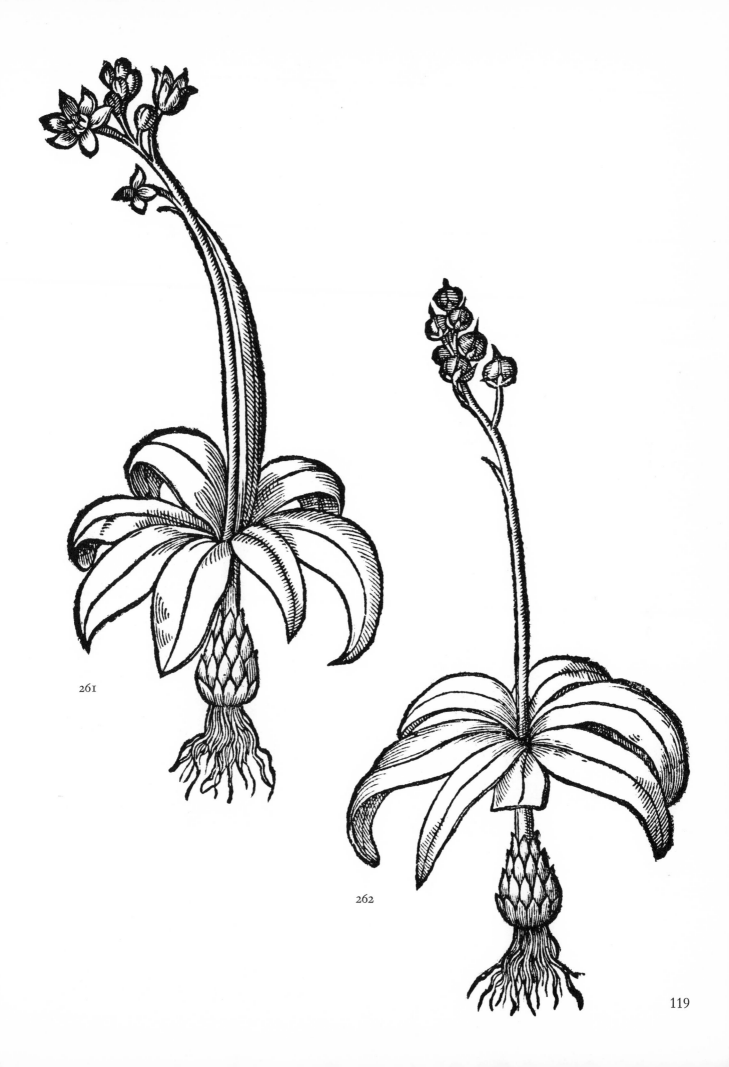

261

262

263

264   265

266

267   268

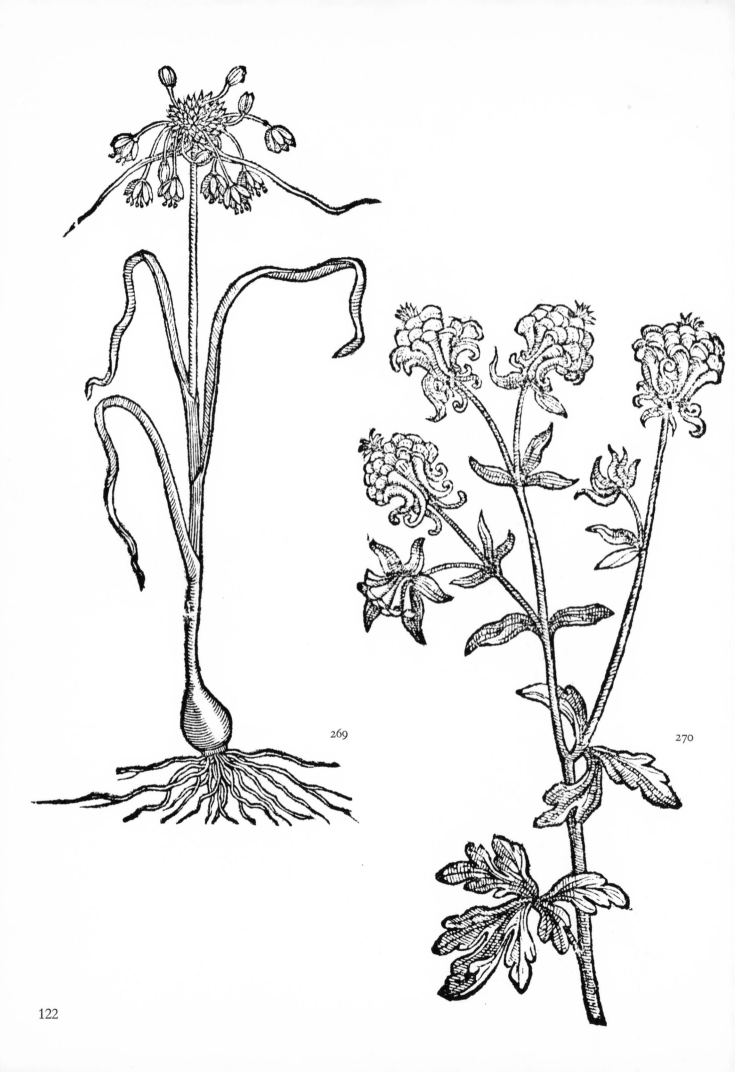

269

270

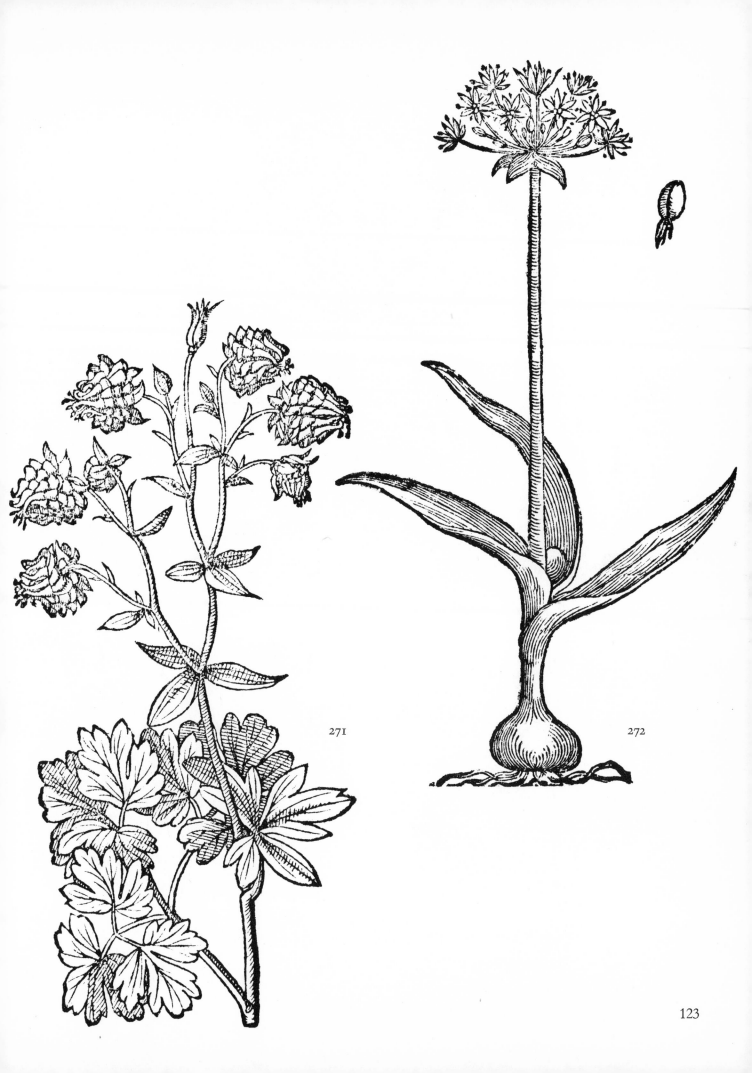

271

272

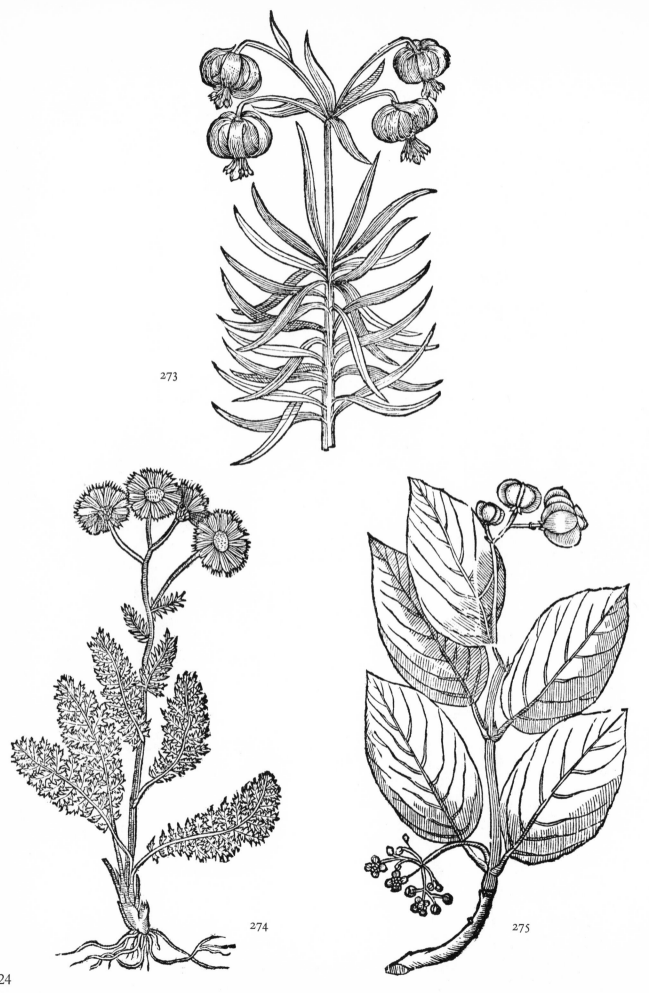

273

274

275

276

277 278

279

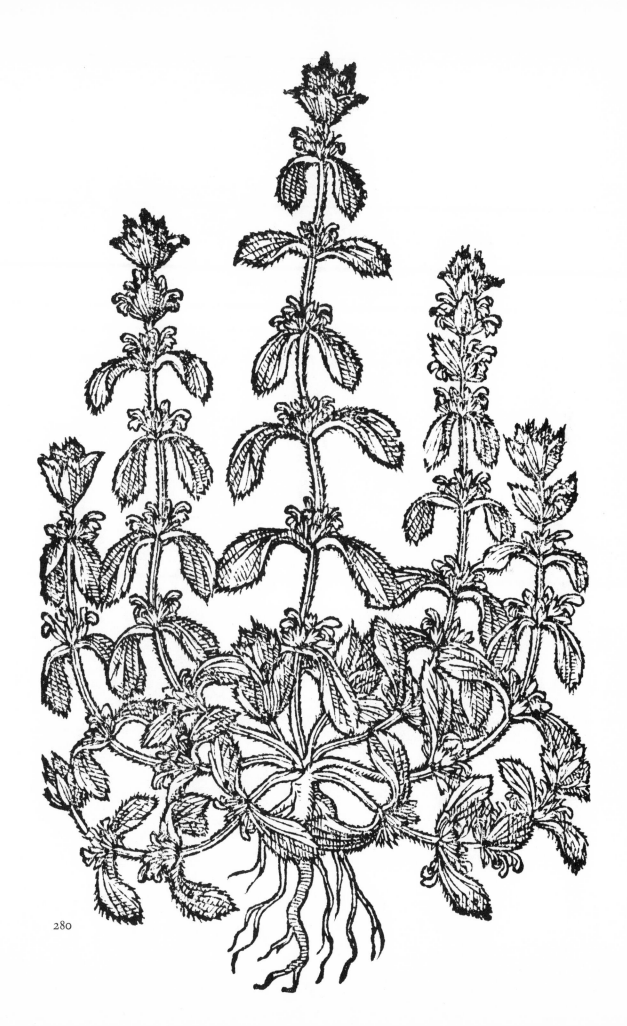

281

282

283

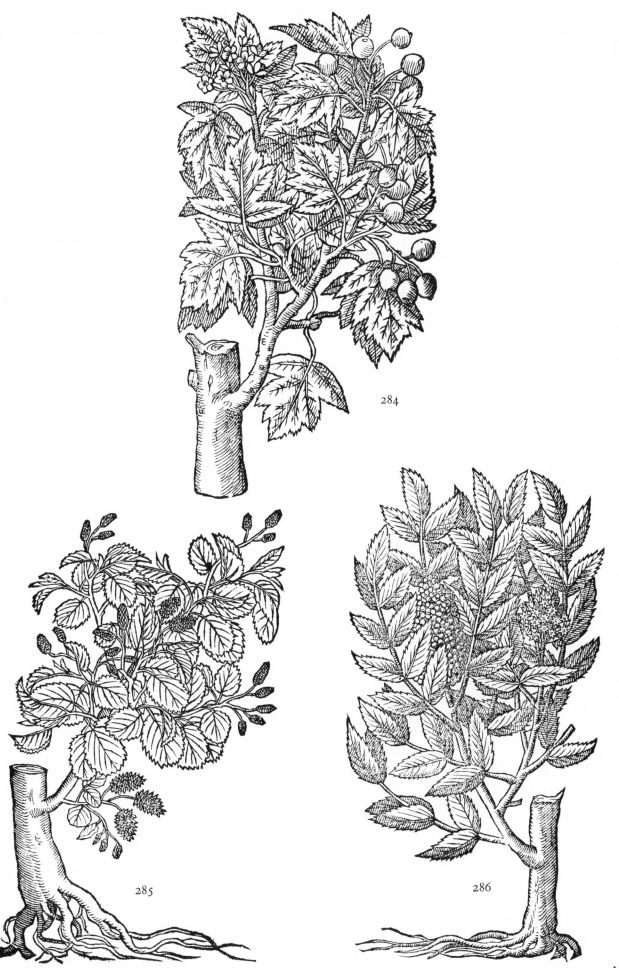

284

285

286

287

288

289

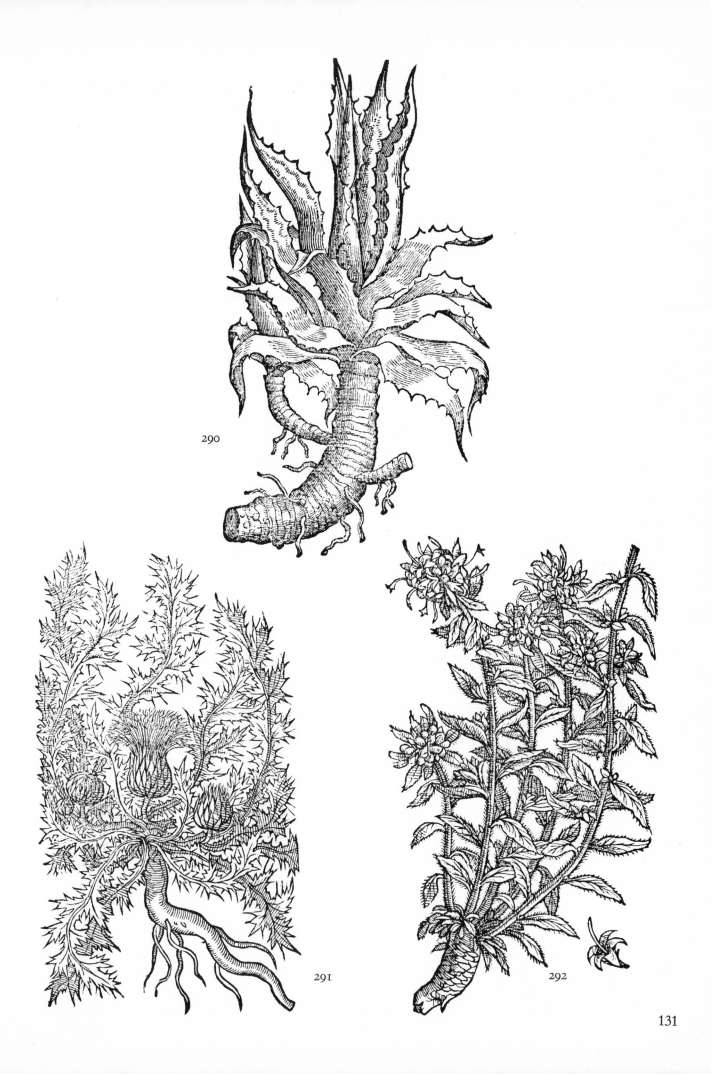

290

291   292

293

294

295

296

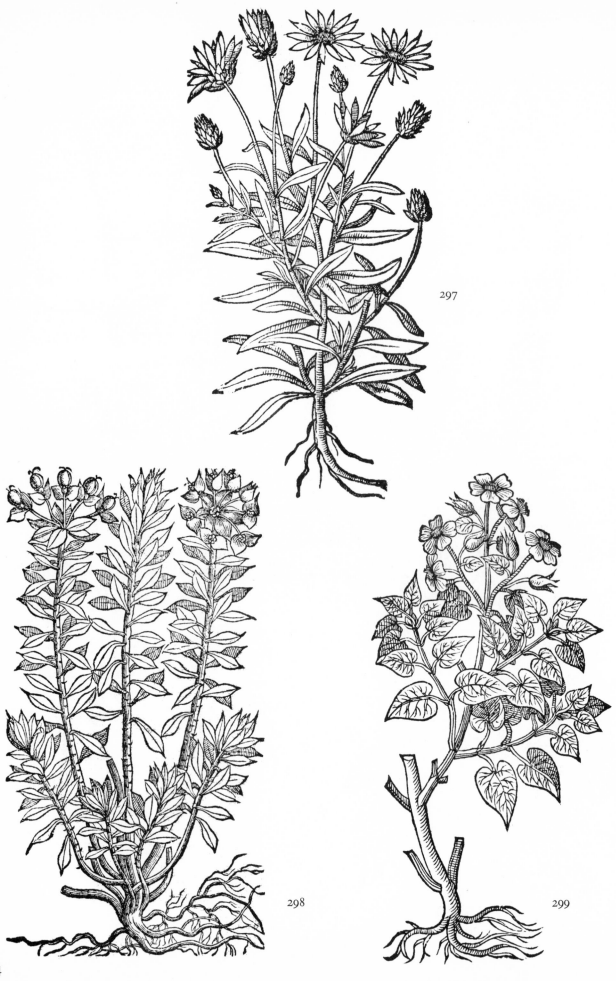

297

298

299

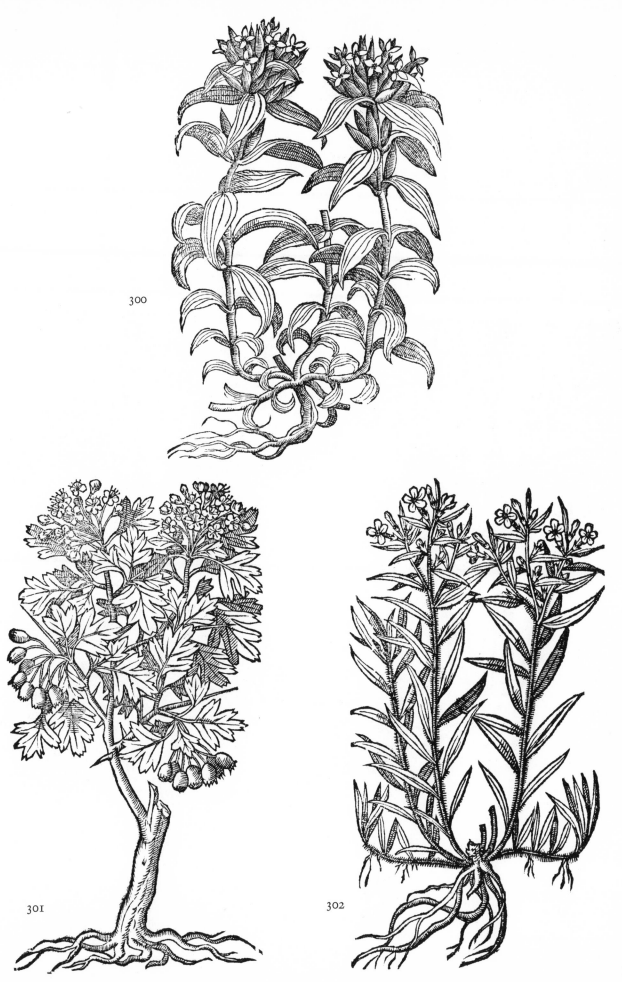

300

301   302

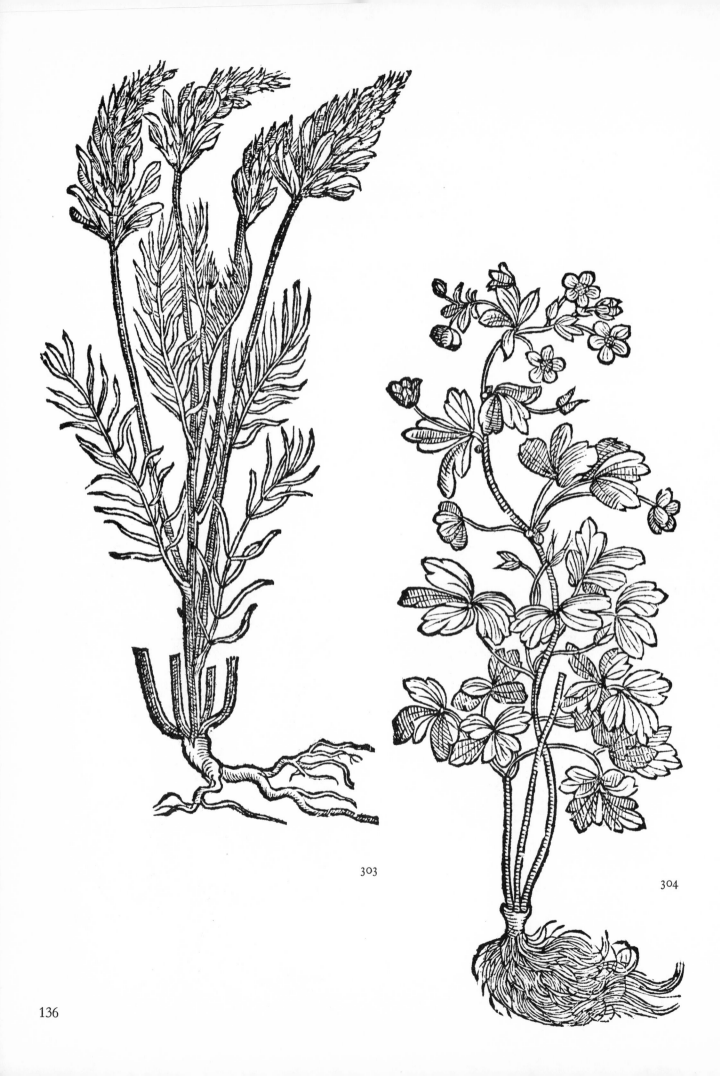

303

304

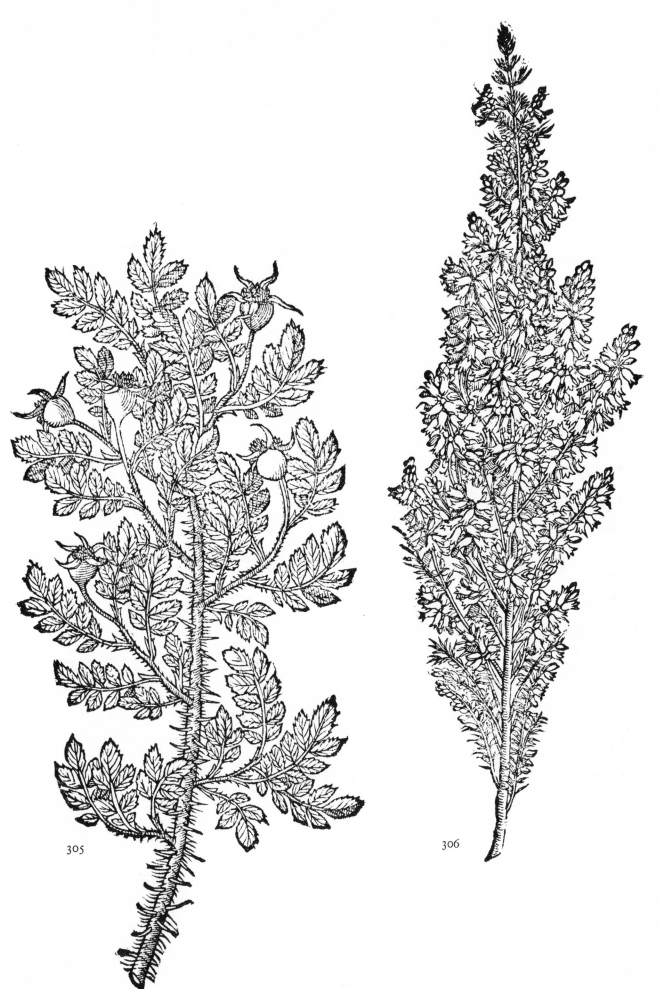

305

306

307

308

309

310

311

312

313

314

315

316

317

318

319

320

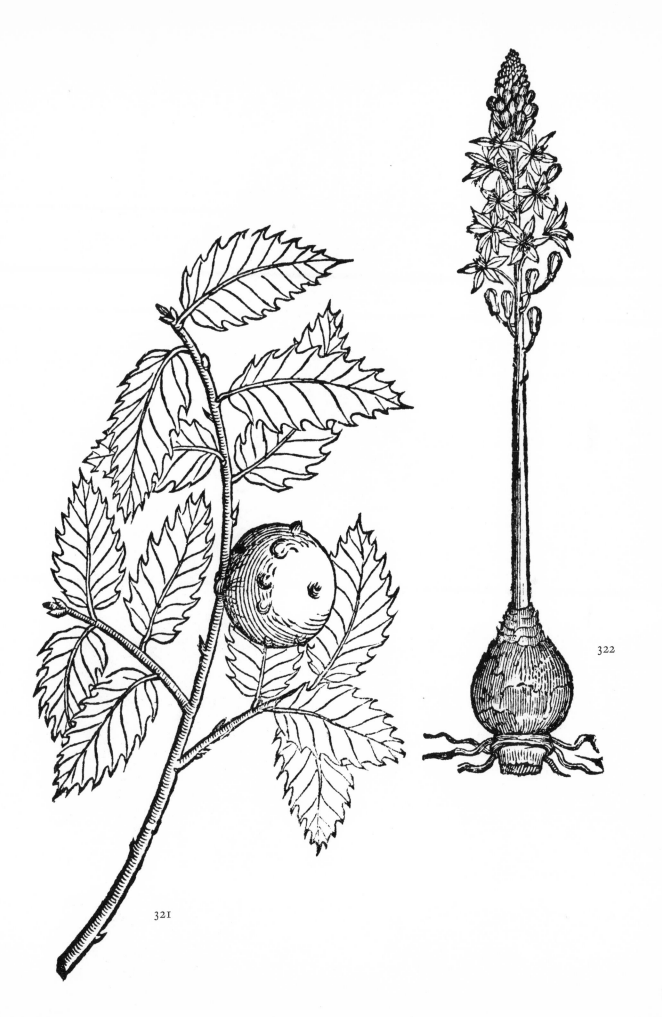

321

322

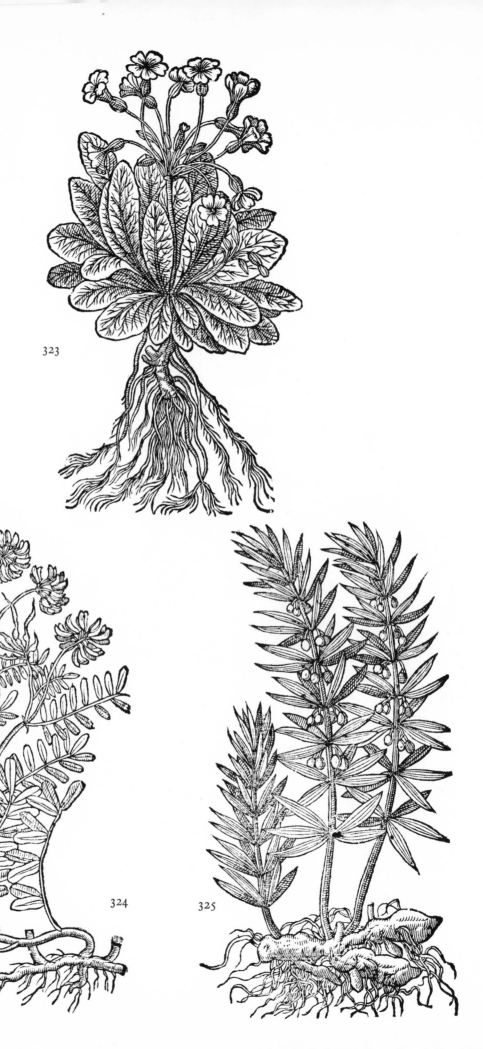

323

324 325

326

327   328

329

330

331

332

333

334

335

336

337

338

339

340

149

341

342

343

344

345   346

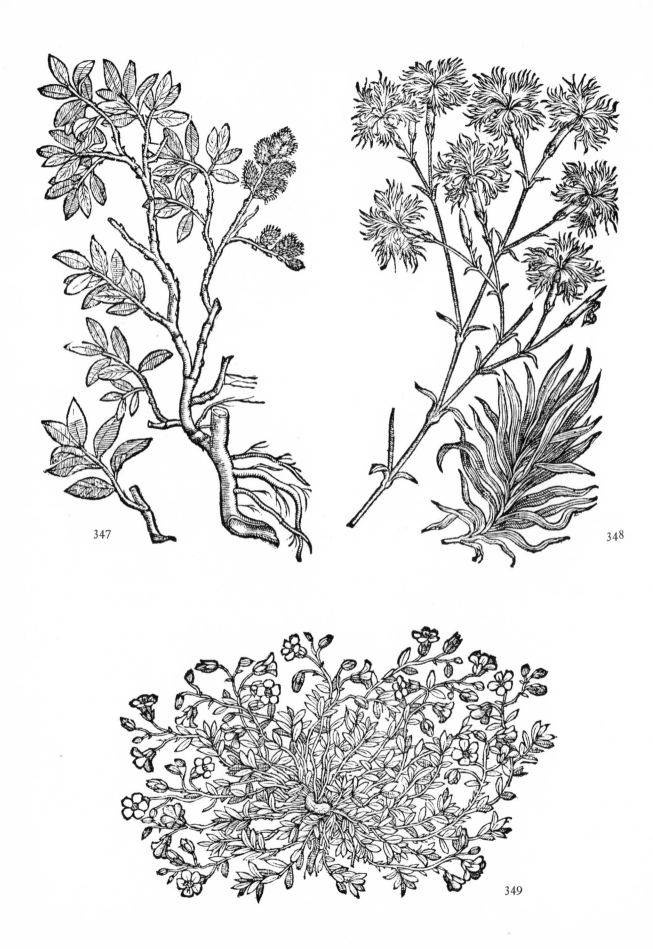

347

348

349

350

351

352

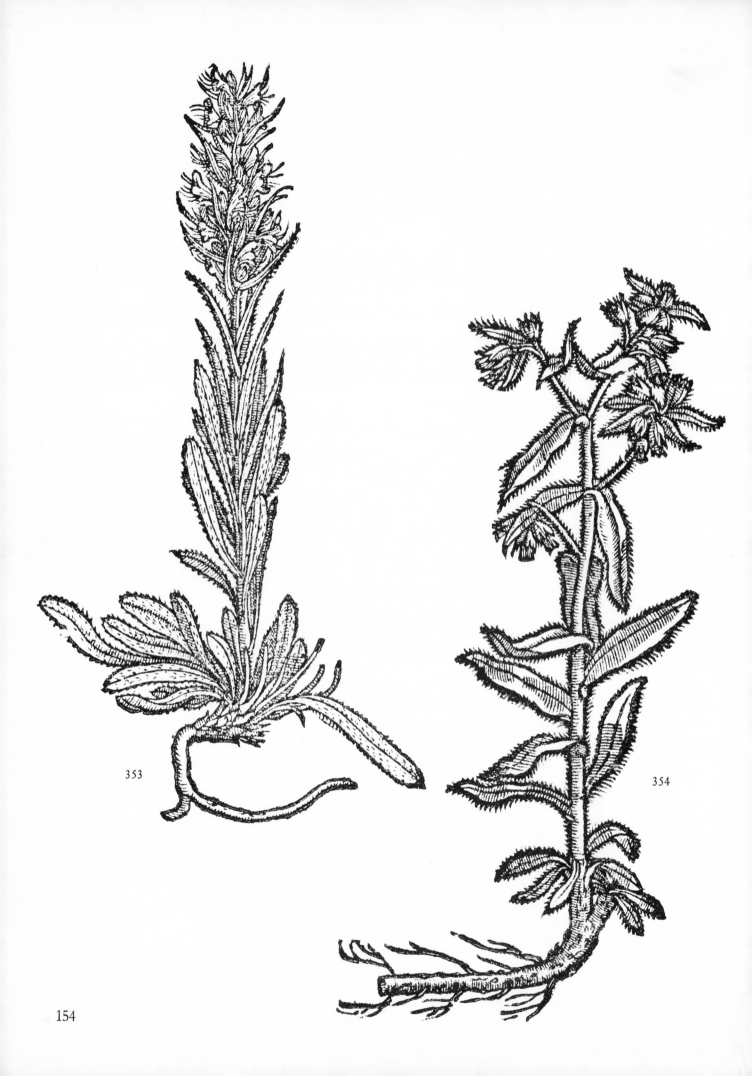

353
354

355

356

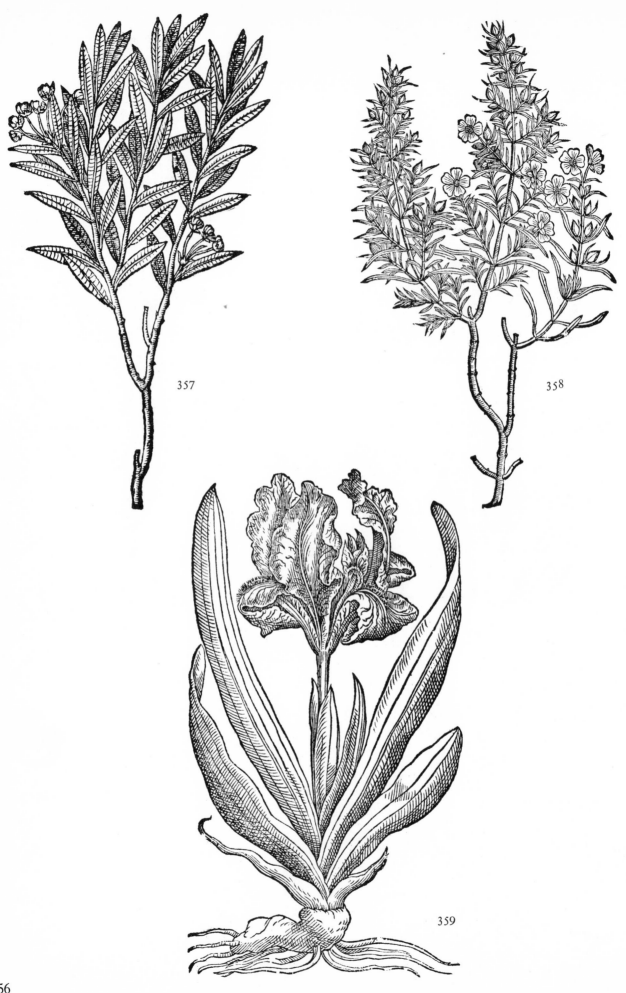

357

358

359

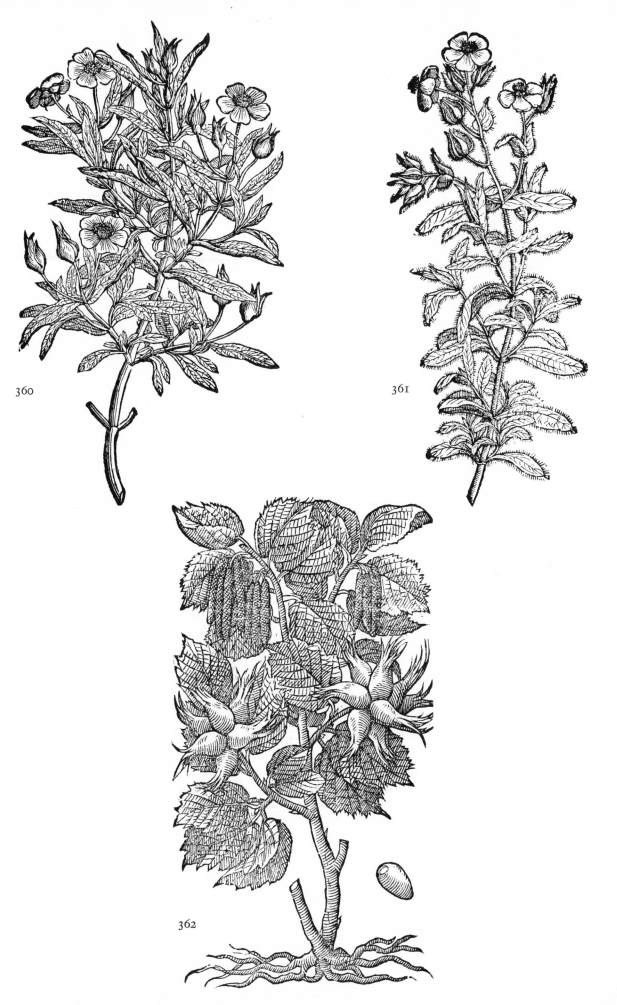

360

361

362

363

364

365

366

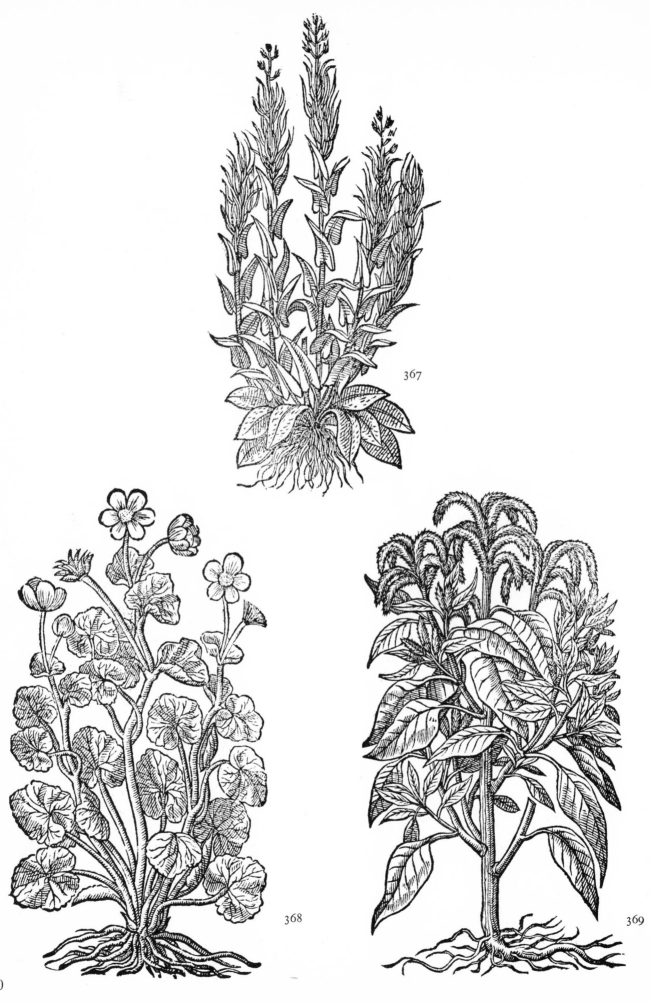

367

368

369

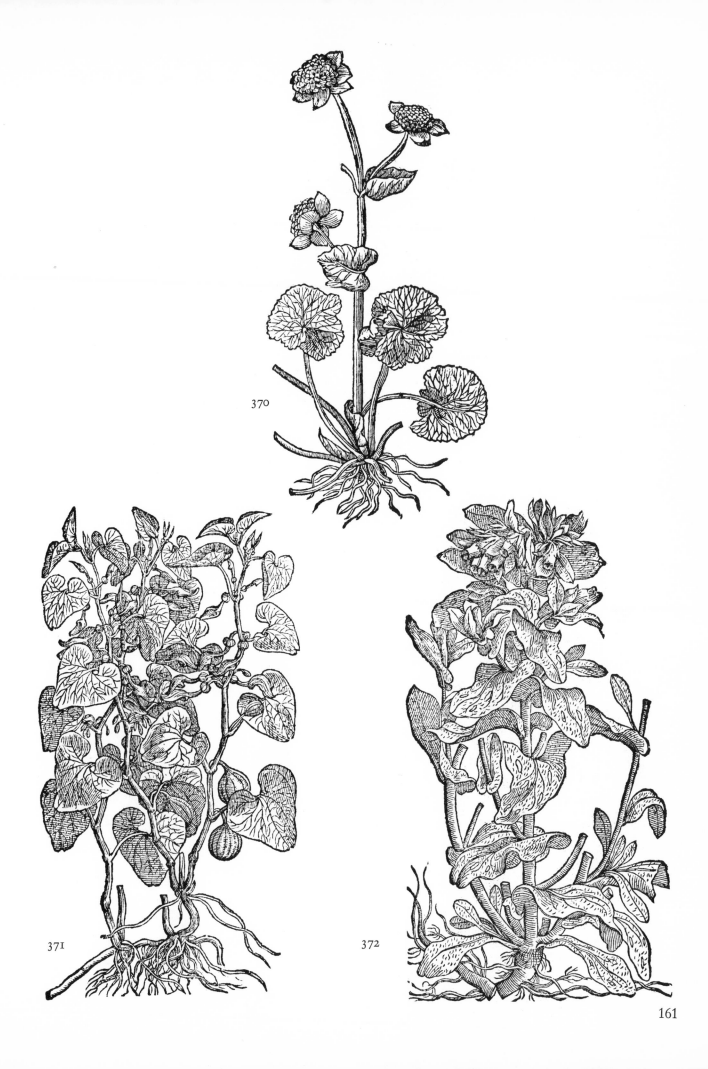

370

371

372

373

374

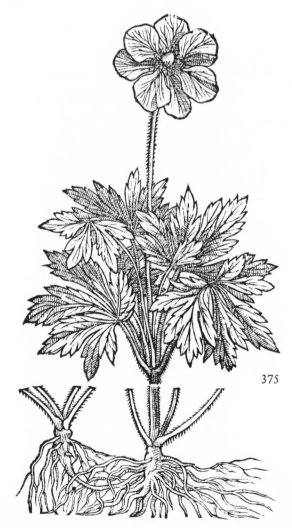

375

376

377   378

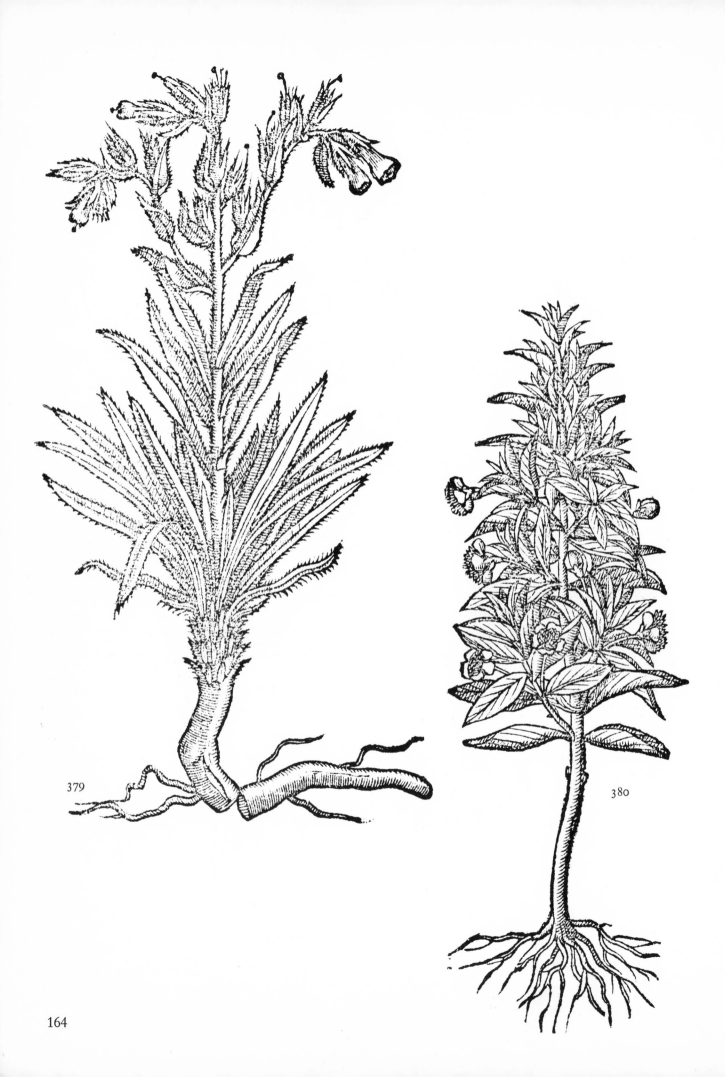

379

380

164

381   382

383

384

385

386

387   388

389   390

391

392

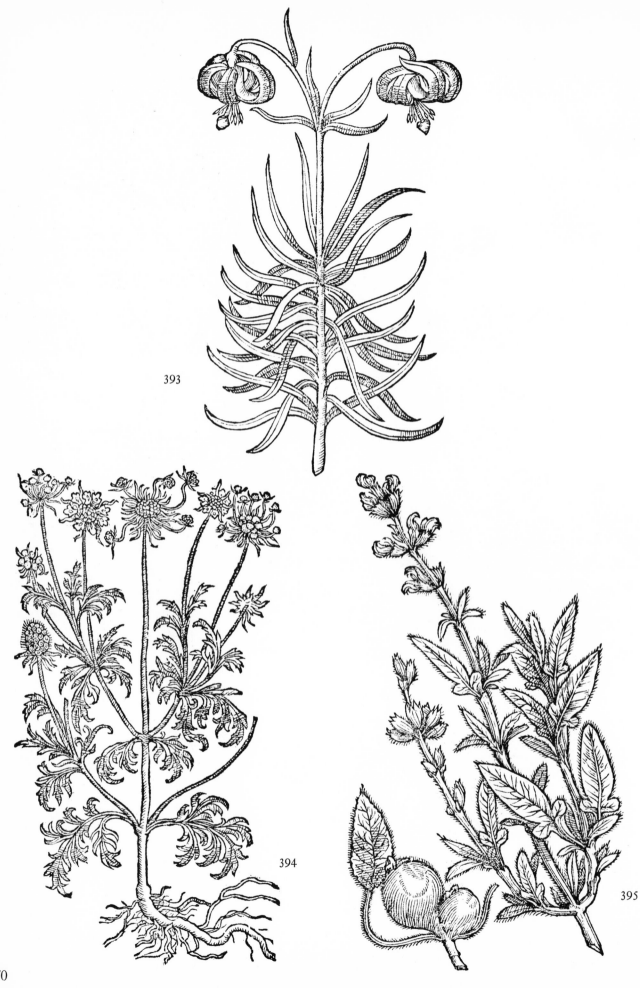

393

394

395

396

397

398

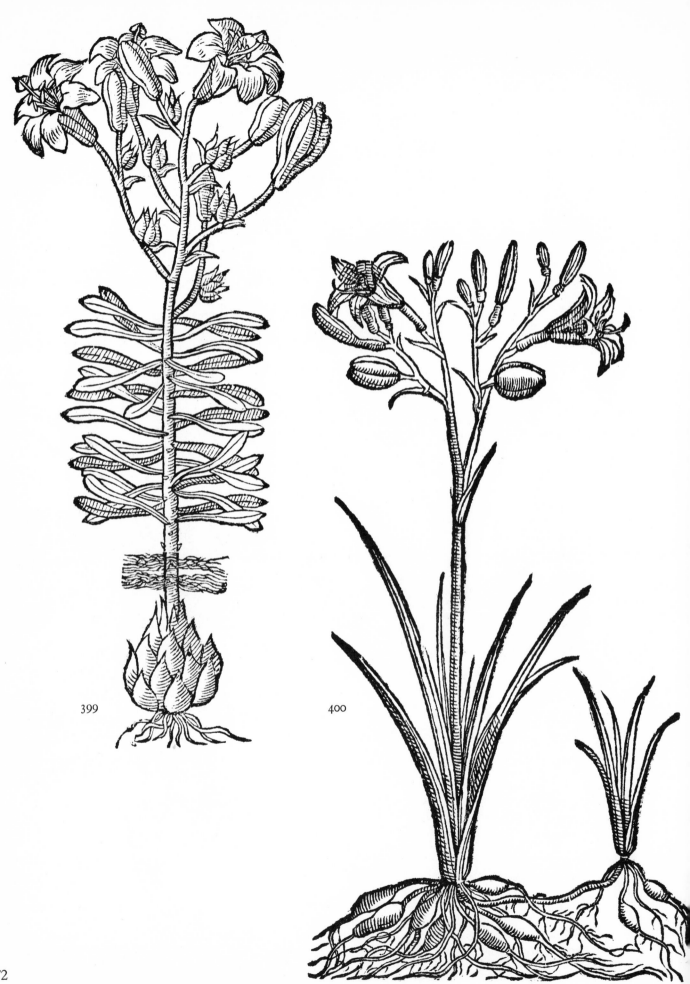

399   400

401

402

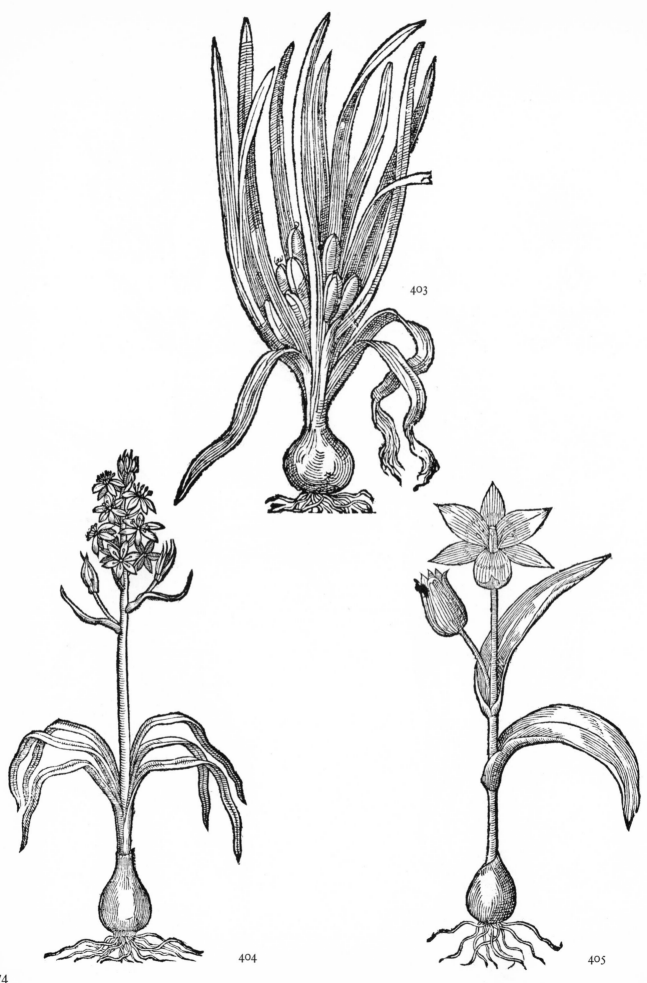

403

404

405

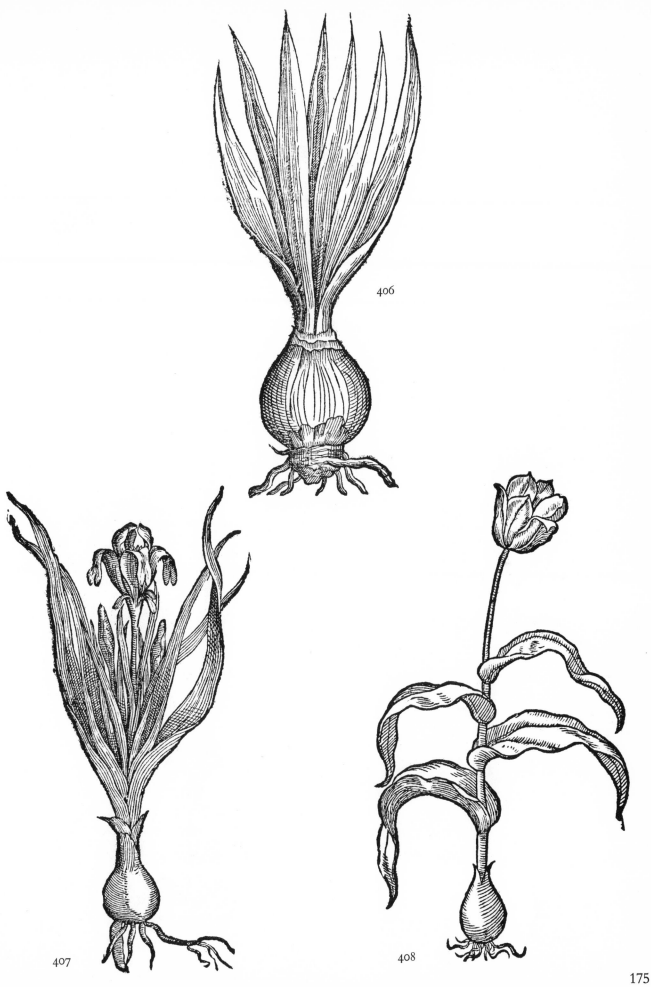

406

407

408

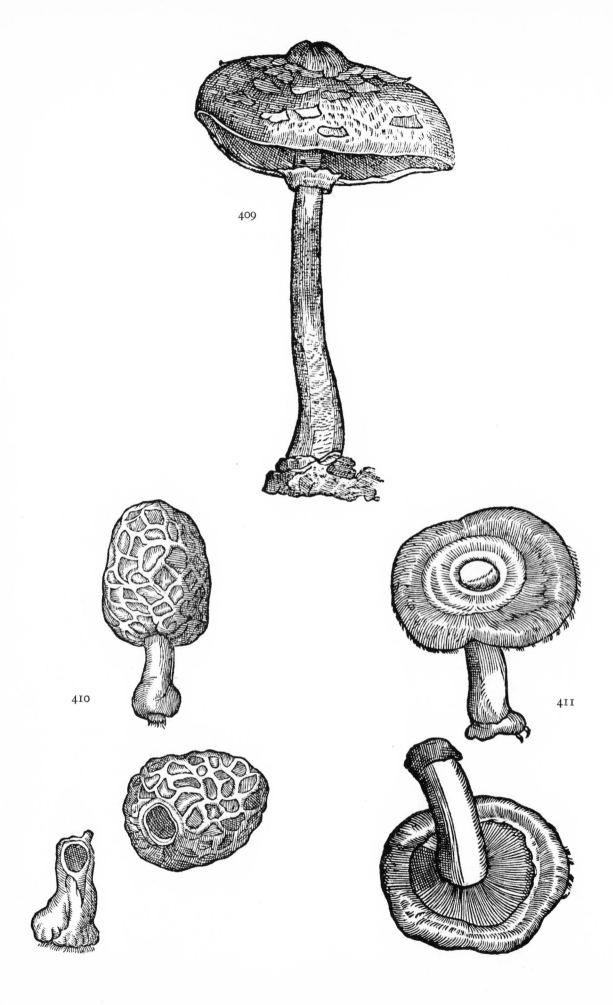

409

410

411

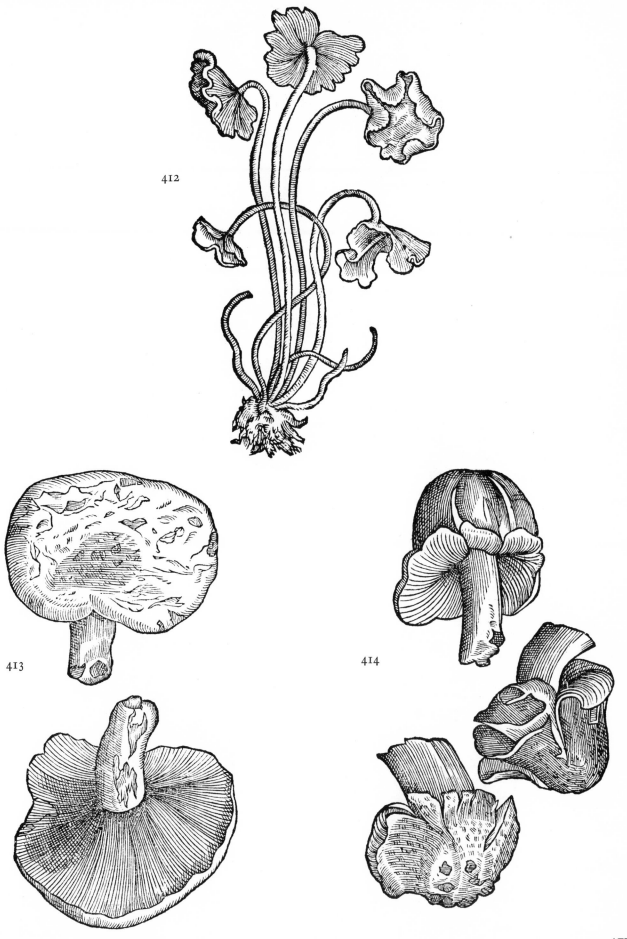

412

413

414

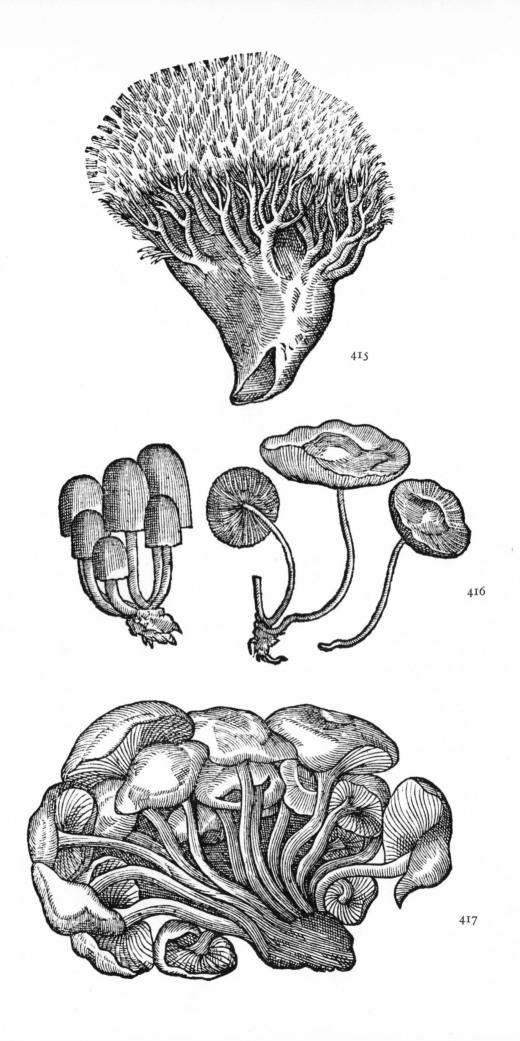

415

416

417

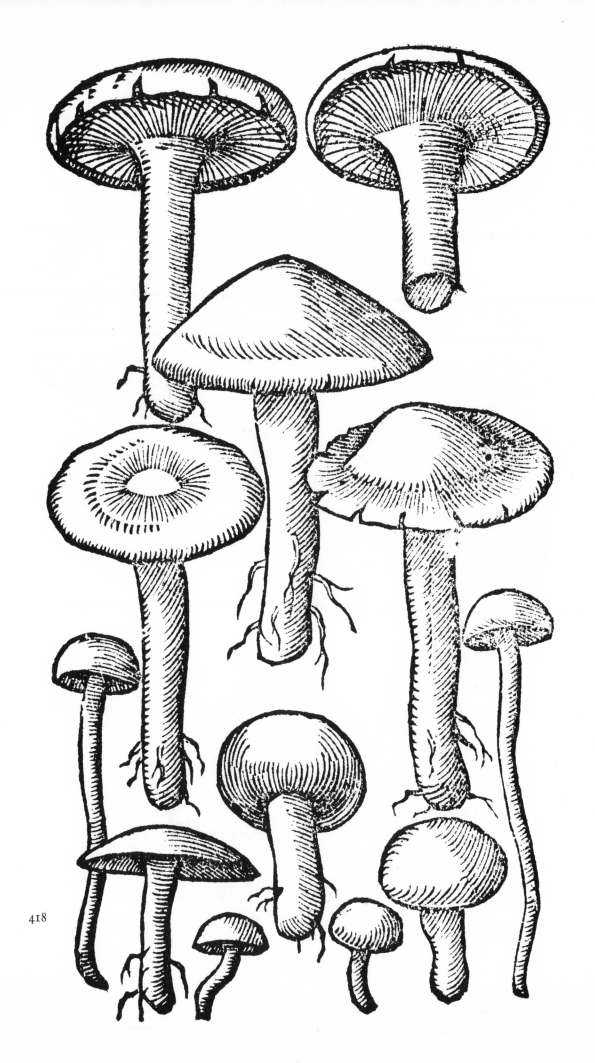

418

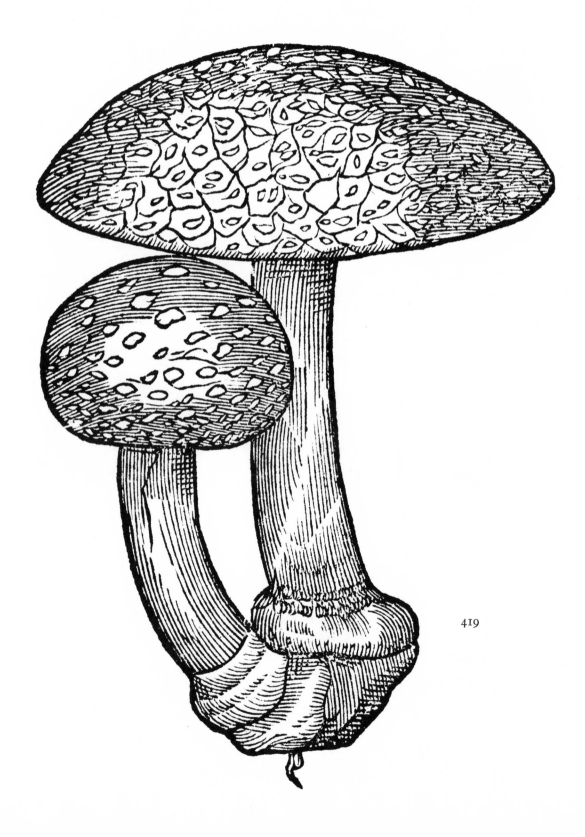

419

List of Plants

The numbers refer to those assigned the figures. The Latin names are those used by Clusius in his captions (see p. v). Brackets indicate identifications and completions of names supplied from Clusius' text.

1. Poma Adami
2. Periclymenum rectum
3. Limones
4. Citria malus
5. Ziziphus alba
6. Malum aureum
7. Ostrys Theophrasti
8. Narcissus
9. Tulipa praecox rubra
10. Tulipa praecox alba
11. Narcissus
12. Iris latifolia major
13. Iris latifolia major
14. Centaurium majus
15. Geranium alpinum longius radicatum
16. Pistolochia
17. Stachys spinosa
18. Cotyledon
19. Stoebe Salmantica
20. Tulipa praecox flava
21. Colchicum Pannonicum
22. Colchicum Byzantinum and Colchicum
23. Tulipa praecox purpurea
24. Ilex coccigera
25. Ilex major
26. Myrto-cistus pennaei
27. Colutea scorpioides altera
28. Ledum silesiacum
29. Rosa campestris
30. Uva ursi
31. Evonymus
32. Tusai, or Lilium Persicum
33. Tusai, or Lilium Persicum
34. Lilium Byzantinum miniatum
35. Teucreum fructicans Baeticum
36. Paeonia Byzantina
37. Iris Asiatica caerulea, or Latifolia major
38. Phaseolus peregrinus
39. Oreoselinum
40. Doronicum Stiriacum
41. Phaseolus peregrinus
42. Scolymus Dioscoridis
43. Lagopus maximus Lobelii
44. Linaria Hispanica
45. Prunella
46. Parthenium alpinum
47. Centaurium parvum
48. Serpillum silvestre Zygis Dioscoridis
49. Campanula lactescens foetidior
50. Polium montanum
51. Anemone hortensis tenuifolia
52. Anemone hortensis tenuifolia
53. Astragalus Mompellianus
54. Anemone hortensis tenuifolia
55. Telephium
56. Hieracium
57. Aster Austriacus
58. Hieracium latifolium
59. Cnius vulgaris
60. Pinaster Hispanicus
61. Abies
62. Pinaster Hispanicus
63. Pinaster Austriacus
64. Fungus esculentus
65. Symphitum tuberosum majus
66. Echium vulgare
67. Avellana pumila Byzantina
68. Anemone hortensis latifolia
69. Fungus esculentus
70. Avellana pumila Byzantina
71. Cytisus
72. Lilium montanum, or Silvestre majus
73. Lilium rubrum praecox
74. Sultan Zambach
75. Martagon bulbiferum
76. Cariophyllata alpina
77. Eriophorus Peruänus
78. Telephium vulgare
79. Parietaria silvestris
80. Victorialis longa
81. Gentiana
82. Iris angustifolia
83. Orchis latifolia
84. Asphodelus minimus
85. Ranunculus grumosa radice
86. Ornithogalum arabicum
87. Trachelium minus
88. Delphinium elatius
89. Laurus Alexandrina Theophrasti
90. Ranunculus montanus
91. Quinquefolium
92. Anagallis
93. Quinquefolium
94. Cytisus
95. Allium, or Moly montanum latifolium
96. Tulipa praecox rubra-varia
97. Tulipa praecox lutea-varia
98. Scorodoprasum
99. Chamaeleon albus Dioscoridis, or Ixia Theophrasti
100. Cirsio congener Card[uus] bulbos[us] Monsp[elliensius]
101. Arisarum latifolium
102. Lotus siliquosus
103. Canna Indica
104. Nymphaea lutea major
105. Batatas

106. Nymphaea alba, or Lotus Aegyptia Alpini
107. Iris angustifolia
108. Scorsonera humilis angustifolia Pannonica
109. Cirsium Anglicum
110. Cotyledon Matthioli
111. Seseli montanum Pannonicum
112. Iris latifolia major
113. Ranunculus Asiaticus grumosa radice
114. Chamaeiris latifolia
115. Chamaeiris latifolia major
116. Iris latifolia major
117. Ranunculus peregrinus grumosa radice
118. Plantago major incana
119. Hepatica trifolia caerul[ea]
120. Spina infectoria pumila
121. Ziziphus rutila
122. Phillyrea
123. Evonymus
124. Securidaca vera
125. Vitis idaea
126. Chamaeiris latifolia minor
127. Ranunculus Creticus latifolius
128. Primula veris humilis
129. Gentiana
130. Horminum silvestre
131. Althaea frutex
132. Colchicum Byzantinum platiphyllon
133. Narcissus autumnalis major
134. Tulipa dubia major
135. Moly Indicum
136. Tulipa Apenninea
137. Narcissus latifolius prorsus
138. Lilium Susianum
139. Anemone hortensis latifolia
140. Paeonia minor
141. Osyris Austriaca
142. Iris latifolia major
143. Allium montani
144. Narcissus latifolius prorsus
145. Tulipa serotina polyclades
146. Tulipa dubia major
147. Tulipa dubia media versicolor
148. Sedum majus legitimum
149. Lysimachia purpurea communis major

150. Elleborus niger legitimus
151. Thlaspi montanum
152. Aconitum Lycoctonum Neubergense
153. Radix cava major
154. Anemone hortensis tenuifolia
155. Anemone hortensis latifolia
156. Hieracium parvum Creticum
157. Leucoium silvestre
158. Iacea Austriaca
159. Pulmonaria Austriaca
160. Cerinthe quorundam major
161. Trifolium majus
162. Pulmonaria Pannonica
163. Cerinthe quorundam minor
164. Pulmonaria vulgaris
165. Alectorolophos alpina
166. Frutex coronarius
167. Caryophyllata vulgaris
168. Cistus femina
169. Campanula Persicae folio
170. Elleborus albus
171. Coronaster forte Gesneri
172. Clinopodium Austriacum
173. Scabiosa, or Aestivalis
174. Scabiosa alba
175. Chrysanthemum alpinum
176. Halimus
177. Lychnis sylvestris latifolia
178. Hesperis
179. Pyrola vulgatior
180. Gentiana
181. Tulipa serotina polyclonos minor
182. Aristolochia Clematitis Baetica
183. Aristolochia rotunda
184. Primula veris elatior
185. Primula veris
186. Smilax aspera
187. Geranium aimatodes
188. Thymum legitimum
189. Althaea vulgaris
190. Linum silvestre latifolium
191. Bulbus Eriophorus
192. Primula veris
193. Tithymalus characias
194. Scorsenera major Hispanica
195. Ranunculus Asiaticus grumosa radice

196. Buphthalmum vul[gare] Chrysant[hemo] cong[ener]
197. Narcissus latifolius prorsus
198. Chrysanthemum Creticum
199. Anemone hortensis tenuifolia
200. Admirabilis Peruäna
201. Cepaea Matthioli
202. Heliotropium minus Tricoccum
203. Asphodelus
204. Phaseolus peregrinus
205. Alyssum minimum
206. Vitis idaea
207. Veronica fructicans
208. Narcissus
209. Narcissus praecox
210. Hyacinthus orientalis
211. Hyacinthus orientalis niveus
212. Auricula ursi
213. Anemone hortensis latifolia
214. Ranunculus silvarum
215. Anemone hortensis latifolia
216. Auricula ursi
217. Anemone hortensis tenuifolia
218. Cortusa Matthioli
219. Chrysanthemum alpinum
220. Aster
221. Tulipa dubia media
222. Cytisus
223. Polygonum Plinii minus
224. Polygonum Plinii majus
225. Picea pumila
226. Auricula ursi
227. Linum silvestre latifolium
228. Iris latifolia major
229. Caryophylleus silvestris
230. Auricula ursi
231. Caryophylleus silvestris
232. Quinquefolium majus
233. Dorycnium Plateau
234. Elichryson
235. Armerius Pannonicus
236. Ribes vulgaris
237. Ledon
238. Hesperis
239. Viola latifolia Lunaria odorata
240. Lamium Pannonicum
241. Hieracium montanum
242. Hieracium villosum
243. Cistus annuus
244. Ledon latifolium majus

245. Casia quorundam
246. Sanicula montana
247. Sanicula montana
248. Phillyrea
249. Genista tinctoria Hispanica
250. Anemone hortensis latifolia
251. Chamaecerasus
252. Lilium montanum
253. Hyacinthus stellatus
254. Cytisus
255. Odontitis Plinii
256. Melandryum Plinii quorundam
257. Tinus
258. Lychnis Byzantina
259. Odontitis Plinii
260. Dentaria major or aphyllos
261. Hyacinthus stellatus Lilii
262. Hyacinthus stellatus Lilii
263. Rosa sine spinis
264. Clematis
265. Atragene Theophrasti
266. Coggygria
267. Pulsatilla vulgaris
268. Pulsatilla vulgaris
269. Allium, or Moly montanum
270. Aquilina
271. Aquilina
272. Moly Theophrasti
273. Lilium montanum
274. Tanacetum inodorum
275. Evonymus latifolius
276. Aquilina degener
277. Tanacetum inodorum
278. Laurocerasus
279. Sideritis
280. Sideritis
281. Acer latifolia
282. Cornus
283. Sorbus legitima
284. Sorbus torminalis Plinii
285. Alnus vulgaris
286. Rhus obsoniorum et
     Coriariorum
287. Aloë
288. Horminum silvestre
289. Telephium
290. Aloë Americana
291. Carlina silvestris
292. Trachelium majus petraeum
293. Anemone hortensis latifolia

294. Phaseolus peregrinus
     angustifolius
295. Rapunculus alopecuriodes
296. Anemone hortensis latifolia
297. Ptarmica Austriaca
298. Tithymalus myrsinites legitimus
299. Ledon latifolium minus
300. Gentiana cruciata
301. Spina appendix Plinii
302. Lithospermum repens majus
303. Onobrichis
304. Ranunculus praecox
305. Rosa campestris
306. Erica
307. Polium
308. Archangelica
309. Caryophyllata montana
310. Geranium bulbosum Pennaei
311. Aconitum lycoctonum
312. Alsine repens major
313. Robur
314. Olea sativa
315. Suber latifolium
316. [Persea]
317. Alnus
318. Laurocerasus
319. Scilla Hispanica
320. Robur
321. Robur
322. Scilla Hispanica
323. Primula veris
324. Securidaca
325. Polygonatum angustifolium
326. Caryophylleus silvestris
327. Ledon
328. Ranunculus montanus
329. Lentiscus
330. Aspalathus
331. Silvestris olea
332. Phillyrea
333. Ledum alpinum
334. Iuniperus alpina
335. Ilex major
336. Tinus
337. Myrica silvestris
338. Alaternus
339. Alaternus
340. Cistus
341. Ranunculus
342. Lychnis silvestris

343. Caryophylleus
344. Anemone silvestris
345. Ranunculus Asiaticus
     polyclonos, or Ranunculus
     grumosa radice
346. Lychnis silvestris
347. Salix pumila latifolia
348. Caryophylleus silvestris
349. Chamaecistus
350. Terebinthus
351. Polygonatum latifolium
     ramosum
352. Chamaecistus
353. Echium
354. Echium
355. Galeopsis maxima Pannonica
356. Lamium Pannonicum
357. Rosmarinus silvestris aosmos
358. Ledon
359. Chamaeiris latifolia minor
360. Cistus mas
361. Ledon
362. Corylus
363. Colutea scorpioeides elatior
364. Lamium Pannonicum exoticum
365. Draba
366. Rhamnus
367. Rhamnus
368. Caltha palustris vulgaris
369. Quinua, or Blitum majus
     Peruänum
370. Caltha palustris
371. Aristolochia Clematitis vulgaris
372. Cerinthe quorundam major
373. Sideritis
374. Caucalis major
375. Anemone silvestris
376. Cardamine alpina trifolia
377. Rosa Cinamomea
378. Doronicum latifolium
379. Anchusa
380. Myrtus Baetica angustifolia
381. Orobus Pannonicus
382. Orobus Pannonicus
383. Iris bulbosa flava-varia
384. Ornithogalum majus
385. Crocum montanum
386. Iris bulbosa, or Iris versicolor
387. Hyacinthus comosus Byzantinus
388. Hyacinthus orientalis polyanthes

389. Ledon
390. Cytisus
391. Cytisus
392. Orobanche polyclonos
393. Lilium montanum
394. Scabiosa
395. Salvia Cretica pomifera
396. Rosa centifolia Batavica
397. Ilex coccigera
398. Geranium Batrachiodes minus
399. Martagon bulbiferum

400. Martagon bulbiferum
401. Pseudo-leimodoron
402. Orchis Pannonica
403. Colchicum Pannonicum
404. Ornithogalum Pannonicum
405. Tulipa Byzantina
406. Bulbus Eriophorus
407. Iris bulbosa latifolia
408. Tulipa serotina flava
409. Fungus esculentus
410. Fungus esculentus

411. Fungus esculentus
412. Fungus Clypeiformis perniciosus
413. Fungus esculentus
414. Fungus esculentus
415. Fungus esculentus
416. Fungus exilis perniciosus
417. Fungus perniciosus
418. Vulgares edules fungi
419. Fungus perniciosus